新开端英语专业基础课系列教材

Extensive Reading
阅读拓展
Yuedu Tuozhan

2
学生用书
（第2版）

总主编　胡　健　戚　涛
主　编　朱玲麟
副主编　张丽红

新开端英语专业基础课系列教材

图书在版编目(CIP)数据

阅读拓展第 2 册学生用书 / 朱玲麟主编 .--2 版 .-- 合肥：安徽大学出版社 , 2025.1
新开端英语专业基础课系列教材 / 陈正发主编
ISBN 978-7-5664-2557-7

Ⅰ.①阅… Ⅱ.①朱… Ⅲ.①英语—阅读教学—高等学校—教材 Ⅳ.① H319.37

中国版本图书馆 CIP 数据核字 (2022) 第 258291 号

出版发行：	北京师范大学出版集团
	安 徽 大 学 出 版 社
	（安徽省合肥市肥西路 3 号 邮编 230039）
	www.bnupg.com
	www.ahupress.com.cn
印　　刷：	安徽利民印务有限公司
经　　销：	全国新华书店
开　　本：	880 mm × 1230 mm　1/16
印　　张：	7.25
字　　数：	207 千字
版　　次：	2025 年 1 月第 2 版
印　　次：	2025 年 1 月第 1 次印刷
定　　价：	28.00 元

ISBN 978-7-5664-2557-7

策划编辑：李　雪	装帧设计：李　军
责任编辑：李　雪	美术编辑：李　军
责任校对：高婷婷	责任印制：陈　如　孟献辉

版权所有　侵权必究

反盗版、侵权举报电话：0551-65106311
外埠邮购电话：0551-65107716
本书如有印装质量问题，请与印制管理部联系调换。
印制管理部电话：0551-65106311

前　言

在信息膨胀、知识爆炸的今天，面对数量庞大、纷繁芜杂的观点和信息，高效获取有价值的信息、辨识和评判各种观点，成了现代人的必备技能。因此，在高等英语教育中，提升学生的阅读能力，尤其是批判性阅读的能力成了一项重要任务，这也对阅读教材的编写提出了更高的要求。作为英语专业的泛读教材，本教材在安徽省"十一五"规划教材《阅读拓展》（1~4册）的基础上进行修订。受时代因素所限，旧版教材存在文字相对陈旧、选材视野不宽、练习较为单调、缺乏思维训练等诸多缺憾。为应对国家培养复合型、创新型高素质英语人才的需求和AI时代提出的新挑战，本团队对旧版教材进行了大幅修改，其中第1册更新比例为70%，其余3册更新比例为100%。最突出的变化是：旧版教材局限在扩大词汇量及提高阅读能力；新版教材则着眼于阅读、批判性思维、跨文化交际、价值观等能力与素养的综合提升，尤其是第3、4册，突出了批判性阅读能力的训练。

教材第1、2册着重介绍英语阅读的常见技巧，旨在帮助学生在保证信息获取准确度的前提下，进一步提升阅读速度，从而提高阅读效率。第1、2册各8个单元，每单元有一个相对独立的主题，介绍一个主要的阅读技巧，包括快速获取主旨大意、通过上下文猜测词义、区分观点与事实等。

第1、2册每单元Lesson A均分为Before Reading、While Reading、After Reading 3个部分。Before Reading部分起到课程导入的作用，形式丰富多样，有传统的课前讨论、词汇头脑风暴，也有新型的思维导图绘制及海报制作等。While Reading部分选材广泛，主题多样，涉及政治、经济、文化、环保、文学、社会等领域。所选文本长度与难度适中，一般为1000词左右，适合课堂教学及学生自学。

Extensive Reading 2

文后配套练习的形式主要包括阅读理解、判断正误、词汇配对、选词填空、读后讨论等，引导和帮助学生完成整个阅读过程。同时为了发挥"以读促写"的作用，部分单元还设计了相关的写作练习。After Reading 部分是学生深度思考和扩展知识的一个重要环节。每单元还安排了扩展练习 Extension Exercise 和素养提升 Value Cultivation 等内容。Value Cultivation 每单元有不同主题，是传扬中国传统美德或其他类型价值正能量的课程思政内容，贴近学生的生活和学习，以"润物细无声"的方式帮助学生树立正确的人生观和世界观。此外，第1、2册还有机融入了跨文化交际意识和能力的培养。对于阅读文本中出现的文化差异、文化常识等内容均配有相应的注释或介绍，目的是在英语学习的基础阶段培养学生对跨文化交际的敏感性及对待文化差异的正确态度。

教材第3、4册在阅读技能提升的基础上，将批判性思维和课程思政融入英语阅读训练中，旨在帮助学生理解、分析和评判各种观点背后隐藏的逻辑，在此基础上学会选择与社会主义核心价值观相协调的价值立场。第3、4册各8个单元，内容涵盖批判性阅读的概念和相关理论、常用批判性阅读策略、基本论证类型和论证逻辑结构、逻辑推理知识以及常见逻辑谬误等，以阅读能力的提高为"驱动力"，旨在全面提升学生的批判性思维能力和英语综合应用能力，使学生能够对作者的观点、态度、假设、论证等进行分析、整合和评判，能够独立思考、提出问题、分析问题、解决问题。

第3、4册每个单元围绕1个批判性阅读相关概念或者策略展开，并提供2篇阅读材料。文章选自英语国家近年来出版的图书与网络材料，或节选自经典英文作品，其中很大一部分来自BBC, *The Economist*, www.nytimes.com, *Time*, *The Washington Post*, *Scientific American* 等知名报刊杂志与网站，题材涉及教育、科技、语言、历史、艺术、文学、文化等诸多领域。文章均经过精挑细选，长度适中，难度相宜，少数地方做了必要的改写与删减。多数单元的理论介绍之后辅以巩固练习。每单元的两篇课文前均有 Preparatory Work 和课文导入，帮助学生调动图式背景，激发阅读兴趣，了解课文重点。文章后的 Notes 帮助学生了解文章背景和相关知识；文章后的练习根据 Bloom 教育目标分类表的 6 个层级，分为 Remembering and Understanding、Reasoning and Analyzing 和 Reflecting and Creating 3 个部分，并着重融入本单元的批判性阅读策略和技巧。3 个部分的练习内容丰富、形式活泼，主要有填空题、是非判断题、选择题、简答题、讨论题、画图题、短文写作等。单元最后有 3 个总结部分。Self-reflection 部分帮助学生反思本单元重难点的掌握情况。Value Cultivation 部分是课程思政内容，结合本单元话题，力求培养学生求真务实、开拓进取的治学态度和科学观，使学生具有高尚的道德情操、健全的人格、较高的人文素养；认同和坚持优秀的中华传统文化，具备辨别东西方文化中不同价值观的基本素质；具有党和国家意识以及社会主义核心价值观，既具有宽广的国际视野又具有爱国主义情怀。Further Reading 部分是拓展阅读推荐，供学生课后进一步拓展相关话题的阅读量和知识面。

  本套教材适合作为英语专业的教材，供第 1 至第 4 学期的教学使用，每学期 1 册。

  本次修订工作由安徽大学戚涛教授、胡健教授主持，全面负责教材的资料筛选、阅读技巧的编排、练习题型和题量的设定，以及定稿前的主审工作。教材编写具体分工如下：第 1 册张丽红老师编写第 1、5、7、8 单元，朱玲麟老师编写第 2、3、4、6 单元；第 2 册张丽红老师编写第 2、4、7、8 单元，朱玲麟老师编写第 1、3、5、6 单元；第 3 册朱蕴轶老师编写第 1、2、3、8 单元，王敏老师编写第 4、5、6、7 单元；第 4 册朱蕴轶老师编写第 1、4、5、8 单元，王敏老师编写第 2、3、6、7 单元。中国科技大学外籍教师 Murray Wayne Sherk 负责后期语言审校工作。

  虽然编写工作历时 2 年，编者也皆为从教多年的高校教师，但我们仍恐教材存在疏漏不妥之处，欢迎同行专家不吝赐教！

编　者

2024 年 7 月

★ CONTENTS ★

Unit 1 Medicine 1
    Reading Skills 2
    Lesson A 3
    Lesson B 8
    Value Cultivation: Read and Reflect 11

Unit 2 Literature 13
    Reading Skills 14
    Lesson A 15
    Lesson B 19
    Value Cultivation: Read and Reflect 25

Unit 3 Psychology 27
    Reading Skills 28
    Lesson A 29
    Lesson B 33
    Value Cultivation: Read and Reflect 36

Unit 4 Science 39
    Reading Skills 40
    Lesson A 42
    Lesson B 46
    Value Cultivation: Read and Reflect 50

Extensive Reading 2

Unit 5 Language 51
  Reading Skills 52
  Lesson A 53
  Lesson B 59
  Value Cultivation: Read and Reflect 62

Unit 6 Chinese Culture 65
  Reading Skills 66
  Lesson A 68
  Lesson B 72
  Value Cultivation: Read and Reflect 76

Unit 7 Tourism 79
  Reading Skills 80
  Lesson A 82
  Lesson B 87
  Value Cultivation: Read and Reflect 91

Unit 8 Artificial Intelligence 93
  Reading Skills 94
  Lesson A 96
  Lesson B 102
  Value Cultivation: Read and Reflect 106

Unit 1

Medicine

Learning Objectives

Types	Lesson A	Lesson B
Reading Skills	Context Clues and Word Meaning: Synonyms and Antonyms	
Theme	Aspects of Traditional Chinese Medicine	Specific Immunity
Vocabulary	TCM	Medicine

Extensive Reading 2

Reading Skills

Synonyms & Antonyms

A synonym is one of two or more words that have the same or similar meaning. When an author uses a difficult word, the author often will also use a more familiar word to make it easy to understand.

Examples:

1. The old man was cantankerous. He was ill-tempered, mean, and extremely quarrelsome.

2. At first, I was doubtful that I could do the job. After one successful week, however, I am much less dubious.

Quite often a writer creates some opposite situation by using an antonym. An antonym is a word of opposite meaning, like *hot vs. cold* or *left vs. right*. Contrast relationships help readers guess the meaning of unfamiliar words.

Examples:

1. The sea lion is a cumbersome animal on land, but in the water, it is one of the most graceful.

2. In contrast to their enjoyment of their country home, the Jones family found it difficult to adjust to urban life.

Exercise: Use synonym or antonym clues to select the best meaning for each of the italic words in the following sentences.

1. Although I did not totally approve of the contest, I *sanctioned* it for the sake of the students in the class.

   A. disapproved   B. approved   C. defied

2. Because I could not afford to purchase the original painting, I purchased a *replica*. An inexperienced eye could not tell the difference.

   A. twin   B. copy   C. original

3. I was shocked by the *audacity* of Bill's request. He is usually a quiet and shy person.

   A. reasoning   B. lavishness   C. boldness

4. Although the professor's lectures are clear and to the point, his test questions are *ambiguous*.

   A. vague   B. ambitious   C. difficult

5. Her remarks were infrequent as well as short and to the point. She was certainly not a *loquacious* woman.

   A. friendly   B. resentful   C. talkative

Lesson A

Before Reading

Directions: *Please read the following three quotes about medicine. Which one impresses you most and why?*

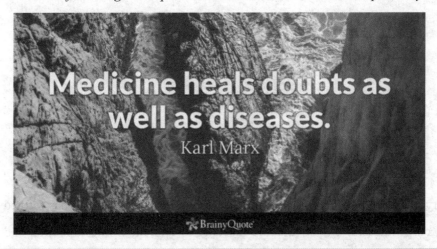

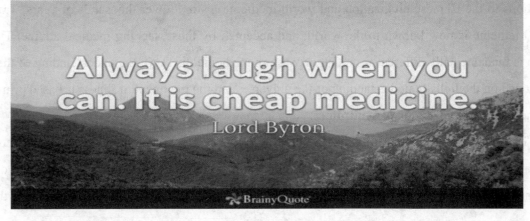

Extensive Reading 2

While Reading

Write down your starting time and ending time, and then calculate your reading rate.

Starting Time: _____   Ending Time: _____

Aspects of Traditional Chinese Medicine

1   With a history of 2000 to 3000 years, Traditional Chinese Medicine (TCM) has formed a unique system to diagnose and cure illness. TCM is valuable heritage of ancient Chinese people, and has made great contributions to the Chinese civilization and world medicine history. Over thousands of years, Traditional Chinese Medicine is now known to the world, and accepted by those seeking medical advice. The TCM approach is fundamentally different from that of Western medicine. In TCM, the understanding of the human body is based on the **holistic** understanding of the universe, and the treatment of illness is based primarily on the diagnosis and differentiation of **syndromes.**

2   The TCM approach treats *zang*-fu organs as the core of the human body. Tissue and organs are connected through a network of channels and blood vessels inside human body. *Qi* (or *chi*) acts as some kind of carrier of information that is expressed externally through *jingluo* system. Pathologically, a dysfunction of the *zang-*

fu organs may be reflected on the body surface through the network, and meanwhile, diseases of body surface tissues may also affect their related *zang* or *fu* organs. Affected *zang* or *fu* organs may also influence each other through internal connections. Traditional Chinese medicine treatment starts with the analysis of the entire system, then focuses on the correction of **pathological** changes through readjusting the functions of the *zang-fu* organs.

3 Evaluation of a syndrome not only includes the cause, mechanism, location, and nature of the disease, but also the confrontation between the pathogenic factor and body resistance. Treatment is not based only on the symptoms, but differentiation of syndromes. Therefore, those with an identical disease may be treated in different ways, and on the other hand, different diseases may result in the same syndrome and are treated in similar ways.

4 The clinical diagnosis and treatment in Traditional Chinese Medicine are mainly based on the *yin-yang* and five elements theories, which belong to the ancient Chinese philosophy. *Yin* and *yang* are the **polarizing** forces naturally in everything. The continuous mutual movement between *yin* and *yang* is the very beginning of the world, and vital for maintaining a balanced universe. Accordingly, if someone gets sick, there must be something wrong with the movements between *yin* and *yang*. And to find out the regular rules of diseases, and obtain satisfactory treatment outcomes, we must know how *yin* and *yang* interplay inside human body. The five elements are metal, wood, water, fire, and earth, each of which generalizes an **attribute** of the objective matter. The theory is that the five elements neutralize and reinforce one another. Based on this, traditional Chinese medicine explains the functional relationship of the vital organs of human body and figures out the solutions when the relationship is out of balance and disease comes.

5 These theories apply the phenomena and laws of nature to the study of the **physiological** activities and pathological changes of the human body and its interrelationships.

Four Diagnostic Methods

6 Bianque, a highly skilled doctor in Spring and Autumn Period, was regarded as a magic doctor in Chinese medicine circle, applied the **comprehensive** diagnostic techniques of traditional Chinese medicines, namely, four diagnostic methods of traditional Chinese medicine: observation, listening, **interrogation**, and pulse-taking. The four diagnostic methods of traditional Chinese medicine make enormous contributions to traditional Chinese medicine, and they are the basic diagnosis methods of traditional Chinese medicine.

7 "Observation" refers to using eyes to observe the patient's look and tongue fur and body fluid (including phlegm, waste, pus, blood etc.) to diagnose the disease. "Listening" refers to listening to the sound of the patient's speech and breath, and smelling the smell of patient's breathing and coughing, which is a reference to diagnosing disease. "Interrogation" refers to asking about the patient's symptoms, and "pulse-taking" is just in the literal meaning that feels the pulse by fingers' touch, through the pulse's location, frequency and

Extensive Reading 2

rhythm etc. to analyze patient's disease.

Typical TCM Therapies

⁸ The typical TCM therapies include acupuncture, herbal medicine, and *qigong* exercises. With acupuncture, treatment is accomplished by stimulating certain areas of the external body. Herbal medicine acts on *zang-fu* organs internally, while *qigong* tries to restore the orderly information flow inside the network through the regulation of Qi. These therapies appear very different in approach yet they all share the same underlying sets of assumptions and insights in the nature of the human body and its place in the universe.

⁹ Nowadays in China, doctors highly value the combination of traditional Chinese Medicine and modern Western medicine. The research shows that the comprehensive treatment of traditional Chinese medicine on a dozen diseases is superior to Western medicine.

¹⁰ Traditional Chinese medicine can be utilized to treat allergies, arthritis pain, and weight control, quitting smoking, back injury pain, musculoskeletal pain, **fatigue** and stress. Other illnesses and conditions that can be helped with traditional Chinese medicine are digestive problems, menstrual problems, urinary problems and even **infertility.**

¹¹ Doctors of TCM suggest all of us to lay greatly emphasis on lifestyle management in order to prevent disease before it occurs. Chinese medicine recognizes that health is more than just the absence of disease and it has a unique capacity to maintain and enhance our capacity for well-being and happiness.

(http://www.tcmpage.com/

874 words; suggested reading time: 8 minutes)

Reading Comprehension

Directions: *Fill in the blanks according to Text A.*

1. Different from Western medicine, TCM is based on the _____ understanding of the universe. That is to say, traditional Chinese medicine treatment starts with the analysis of the entire system.

2. Treatment is not based only on the symptoms, but _____ of syndromes. Therefore, those with an identical disease may be treated in different ways and, on the other hand, different diseases may result in the same syndrome and be treated in similar ways.

3. Typical TCM therapies include _____, _____, and _____.

4. Four diagnostic methods of traditional Chinese medicine: _____, _____, _____, and _____.

5. If someone gets sick, there must be something wrong with the movements between _____ and _____.

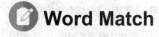

Word Match

Directions: *Match the following words with their definitions.*

Unit 1 Medicine

Group 1: Adjectives

1. holistic ( )	A. causing magnetic or electric polarity in a body or system
2. pathological ( )	B. of or consistent with an organism's normal functioning
3. polarizing ( )	C. including all, or almost all, the items, details, facts, information, etc., that may be concerned
4. physiological ( )	D. treating the whole person rather than just the symptoms of a disease
5. comprehensive ( )	E. caused by, or connected with, disease or illness

Group 2: Nouns

1. syndrome ( )	A. a feeling of being extremely tired, usually because of hard work or exercise
2. attribute ( )	B. someone's lack of the physical ability to have children
3. interrogation ( )	C. a quality or feature of somebody or something
4. fatigue ( )	D. the process of asking someone many questions in order to get information
5. infertility ( )	E. a set of physical conditions that show you have a particular disease or medical problem

Cloze

Directions: *Fill in each blank with the proper form of one of the words given below.*

implementation	mainstream	cold	booming	uncommon
ancient	bump	recommendations	reference	herbal

Traditional Chinese Medicine also called "TCM", is the ___1___ system of traditional medicine developed in China over thousands of years. Although seeking TCM treatment is still somewhat ___2___ in the West, it's hard to spend much time in China without realizing that TCM still enjoys a ___3___ popularity there. Walk down any street and you're likely to ___4___ into several pharmacies selling traditional Chinese ___5___ medicines. You're also likely to hear Chinese people make frequent ___6___ to TCM-related concepts, like the idea that certain foods are "hot" while others are "___7___". Chinese doctors and dentists practicing Western medicine in ___8___ hospitals and clinics may even make TCM-inspired ___9___, focusing on the ___10___ of certain daily living habits to encourage well-being.

Extensive Reading 2

After Reading

Topics for Discussion.

1. What are the major differences between TCM and Western medicine?

2. Have you ever experienced any TCM therapy? Which one do you think is especially effective for you?

Lesson B

Write down your starting time and ending time, and then calculate your reading rate.

Starting Time: _____   Ending Time: _____

Specific Immunity

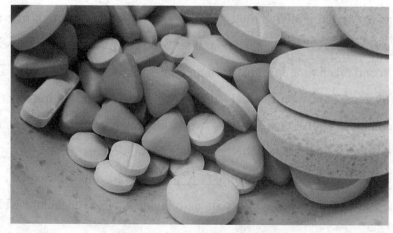

1   Although immunobiology is a relatively recent scientific discipline, the concept of immunity as a means

of resistance to infection is an ancient one. Since the time of the Greeks, it has been recognized that those who recover from plague, smallpox, yellow fever, and various other infectious diseases rarely contract the same disease again.

² The first scientific attempts at artificial immunization were made in the late eighteenth century by the English physician Edward Jenner. Jenner investigated the basis for the widespread belief of peasants in the rural areas in England that anyone who had had vaccinia, or cowpox (from the Latin *vacca* "cow"), a disease that affected both dairy cattle and humans, never contracted smallpox. Smallpox was not only often fatal—10 to 40 percent of those who contracted it died, and children were especially susceptible—but those that recovered usually had disfiguring pockmarks. Yet most British milkmaids, who were readily infected with cowpox, had clear skins because cowpox was a relatively mild infection that left no scars.

³ After some 20 years of close observation, including several deliberate attempts to give smallpox to people who had contracted cowpox, Jenner began to immunize people by deliberately infecting them with cowpox. His first subject was a healthy, eight-year-old boy known never to have had either of these two related diseases. As Jenner had expected, immunization with the cowpox virus caused only mild symptoms in the boy. When Jenner subsequently inoculated him with smallpox virus, the boy showed no symptoms of the disease. Jenner subsequently inoculated patients in large numbers with cowpox pus, as did other physicians in England and on the European continent. By 1800, the practice, known as vaccination, had begun in America, and by 1805, Napoleon commanded all French soldiers to be vaccinated.

⁴ Further work on immunization was carried out by Louis Pasteur (1822-1895), the French physician who established the scientific basis for the germ theory of disease (the fact that microorganisms are responsible for disease) and developed techniques for the maintenance and growth of bacteria in test tubes. Pasteur discovered that neglected, old cultures of chicken cholera bacilli, which had not been placed in a fresh culture medium on a regular basis, produced only a mild attack of this disease in chickens inoculated with it. He then discovered that fresh cultures of the bacteria failed to produce the disease in any chickens that had been previously inoculated with such old cultures. The organisms in the old cultures had somehow become less pathogenic, or <u>attenuated</u>. They had lost their ability to cause damage to cells and tissues, a change that Pasteur later found he could regularly produce in cultures of other kinds of aerobic bacteria by growing them for long periods of time under anaerobic conditions. To honor Jenner, Pasteur gave the name vaccine to any preparations of a weakened pathogen, or infective microbes, that was used as Jenner's "vaccine virus" to immunize against infectious disease.

⁵ Pasteur used vaccination to protect animals against anthrax and people against rabies. Following Pasteur's discovery, other investigations showed that not only weakened, living microorganisms but also microorganisms killed by treatment with formalin, merthiolate, phenol, or heat could induce immunity.

Extensive Reading 2

(517 words; suggested reading time: 6 minutes)

Reading Comprehension

Directions: *Choose the best answer from the four alternatives for the following questions.*

1. Edward Jenner developed a method of artificial immunization against _____.

   A. smallpox   B. cowpox   C. polio

2. The language used in the passage is _____.

   A. informal   B. scholarly   C. argumentative

3. Louis Pasteur developed vaccines to protect _____.

   A. cows against cowpox and people against smallpox

   B. people against typhoid and polio

   C. animals against anthrax and people against rabies

4. What is the meaning of "attenuated" in the Para. 4?

   A. Strengthened.   B. Became weaker.   C. Became useless.

Word Formation

Directions: *Fill in each of the blanks with the given word in its proper form.*

1. AIDS lowers the body's _____ to infection. (resist)
2. _____ are well under way for a week of special events in May. (prepare)
3. The explosion had _____ the building's foundation. (weak)
4. Two dogs attacked him, leaving him horribly _____. (disfigure)
5. The data can _____ be loaded on a computer for processing. (subsequent)
6. The government has promised a full _____ into the disaster. (investigate)
7. He _____ misled us about the nature of their relationship. (deliberate)
8. The cause of the crash was given as engine _____. (fail)

Extension Activity

Directions: *Conduct a classroom debate concerning whether to have mandatory immunization for children before entering school.*

Value Cultivation: Read and Reflect

中医药传承创新发展
The Preservation and Innovative Development of TCM

President Xi said, "More efforts should be made in exploring the essence of TCM and better collaboration between enterprises, universities and research institutes to advance the industrialization, modernization and globalization of TCM."

Keywords

防病治病 disease prevention and treatment

中医药现代化、产业化 modernization and industrialization of TCM

中西医并重 equal importance should be placed on both TCM and Western medicine

Unit 2

Literature

Learning Objectives

Types	Lesson A	Lesson B
Reading Skills	Context Clues and Word Meaning: Example Clues	
Theme	Essay	Short Stories
Vocabulary	Reading	Love

Reading Skills

Context Clues and Word Meaning: Example Clues

Example refers to an individual phenomenon taken as representative of a type, or to a part representative of the whole.

Example clues provide examples or instances that help define the unfamiliar word.

Examples:

1. Many forms of precipitation, such as rain, snow, and hail, contribute to the water cycle.

Rain, snow, and hail are examples of "*precipitation*", giving a clue as to what the term means.

2. There are many different arthropods, such as spiders, crabs, and beetles.

The examples of spiders, crabs, and beetles let you infer that "*arthropods*" are a type of animal with jointed limbs.

Limitations of Context Clues

While context clues are useful for understanding unfamiliar words, they do have some important limitations. For example, context clues are not always present. In these cases, readers need to be able to find other ways to obtain meaning (such as using a dictionary!). Furthermore, there tends to be ambiguity within context clues, especially when the authors' writing is vague. This may lead to multiple possible meanings that could be inferred from the surrounding context, causing confusion. Therefore, it is wise to use context clues flexibly and appropriately.

Exercise: Use example clues to figure out the meaning of the underlined word in the following sentences.

1. There were several types of <u>gymnosperms</u> in the park, such as pines, firs, and spruces.

2. He enjoyed many different <u>genres</u> of music, including rock, jazz, and classical.

3. Her collection of <u>antiquities</u> included artifacts like pottery, coins, and jewelry from ancient civilizations.

4. The children were able to observe several <u>crustaceans</u>, including crabs, lobsters, and shrimp.

5. <u>Constellations</u>, such as The Little Dipper and The Big Dipper, can be seen in the night sky.

6. Fish, whales, and dolphins are <u>aquatic</u> animals.

7. <u>Vicissitudes</u>, such as circumstances, developments, or journeys in life, can change a person forever.

8. A <u>sleuth</u>, such as Sherlock Holmes, can be very helpful in solving crimes.

9. The lawyer had <u>tangible</u> evidence, such as a hammer, a car, and keys, to show that the person stole the car.

10. Zack was good at many sports. He excelled in swimming, running, horsemanship, fencing, and target shooting. He decided to compete in the <u>pentathlon</u> rather than having to choose one of the events.

Lesson A

Before Reading

Directions: *Read the following quotes and work in pairs to translate them into Chinese.*

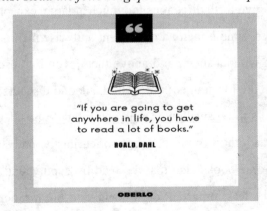

While Reading

Write down your starting time and ending time, and then calculate your reading rate.

Of Studies

Francis Bacon

"Studies serve for delight, for ornament, and for ability. Their chief use for delight is in privateness and retiring; for ornament, is in discourse; and for ability, is in the judgment and disposition of business. For expert men can execute, and perhaps judge of particulars, one by one; but the general counsels, and the plots and marshalling of affairs, come best from those that are learned. To spend too much time in studies is sloth; to use them too much for ornament, is affectation; to make judgment wholly by their rules, is the humor of a scholar. They perfect nature, and are perfected by experience: for natural abilities are like natural plants, that need pruning, by study; and studies themselves do give forth directions too much at large, except they be bounded in by experience. Crafty men condemn studies, simple men admire them, and wise men use them; for they teach not their own use; but that is a wisdom without them, and above them, won by observation. Read not to contradict and confute; nor to believe and take for granted; nor to find talk and discourse; but to weigh and consider. Some books are to be tasted, others to be swallowed, and some few to be chewed and digested; that is, some books are to be read only in parts; others to be read, but not curiously; and some few to be read wholly, and with diligence and attention. Some books also may be read by deputy, and extracts made of them by others; but that would be only in the less important arguments, and the meaner sort of books, else distilled books are like common distilled waters, flashy things. Reading maketh a full man; conference a ready man; and writing an exact man. And therefore, if a man write little, he had need have a great memory; if he confer little, he had need have a present wit: and if he read little, he had need have much cunning, to seem to know that he doth not. Histories make men wise; poets witty; the mathematics subtle; natural philosophy deep; moral grave; logic and rhetoric able to contend. *Abeunt studia in mores* [Studies pass into and influence manners]. Nay, there is no stone or impediment in the wit but may be wrought out by fit studies; like as diseases of the body may have appropriate exercises. Bowling is good for the stone and reins; shooting for the lungs and breast; gentle walking for the stomach; riding for the head; and the like. So if a man's wit be wandering, let him study the mathematics; for in demonstrations, if his wit be called away never so little, he must begin again. If his wit be not apt to distinguish or find differences, let him study the Schoolmen; for they are *cymini sectores* [splitters of hairs]. If he be not apt to beat over matters, and to call up one thing to prove and illustrate another, let him study the lawyers' cases. So every defect of the mind may have a special receipt.

(512 words; suggested reading time: 5 minutes)

Reading Comprehension

Directions: *Answer the following questions.*

1. What are the views of Francis Bacon regarding studies in his essay "Of Studies"?
2. Explain the line "Some books are to be tasted, others to be swallowed, and some few to be chewed and digested" in reference to the context.
3. What are the three main benefits of studies Bacon mentions in this essay?
4. What are the dangers associated with each benefit?
5. Explain Francis Bacon's perspective in the line, "writing (makes) an exact man". Do you agree with him? Why or why not?

Word Formation

Directions: *Fill in each of the blanks with the given word in its proper form.*

1. Thatched pavilions provide shady retreats for relaxing and reading in _____. (private)
2. Richard was _____ the doctors and nurses, showing them where to go. (marshal)
3. He will have a car at his _____ for the whole month. (dispose)
4. Lawson writes so well: in plain English, without fuss or _____. (affect)
5. A sapling needs _____; a child, discipline. (prune)
6. A common saying goes, "Knit the brows and you will hit upon a stratagem." In other words, much thinking yields _____. (wise)
7. She has some interesting _____ on possible future developments. (observe)
8. No liquids are served with meals because they interfere with _____. (digest)
9. The level of inflation is a serious _____ to economic recovery. (impede)

Extensive Reading 2

10. I just want a good reliable car, nothing _____. (flash)

Cloze

Directions: *Fill in each blank with the proper form of one of the words given below.*

| hungry | dive | safely | down | genre |
| local | classical | incredible | invested | replicate |

Have you ever read a book that you couldn't put ___1___?

Do you remember feeling so ___2___ in the story or what you were learning that you would keep reading even when you needed to use the bathroom or were ___3___?

To ___4___ that feeling, or to experience it for the first time, all you need to do is find the right books to read.

There are millions of ___5___ books out there, and there's a perfect reading ___6___ for everyone—from fantasy novels and ___7___ literature to self-help guides and business books.

Reading is something you can enjoy ___8___ at home. And books don't cost that much—especially with services like your ___9___ library and Amazon's Kindle Unlimited.

So, step away from your smartphone each day, open the pages of a book, and ___10___ in.

After Reading

Topics for Discussion.

1. In the essay, Bacon discusses the benefits of reading and the benefits of reading different subjects. Do you agree with him?
2. What are your own approaches to the study of different subjects?

Lesson B

Write down your starting time and ending time, and then calculate your reading rate.

Starting Time: _____   Ending Time: _____

The Gift of the Magi

O. Henry

1   One dollar and eighty-seven cents. That was all. And sixty cents of it was in pennies. Pennies saved one and two at a time by bulldozing the grocer and the vegetable man and the butcher until one's cheeks burned with the silent imputation of parsimony that such close dealing implied. Three times Della counted it. One dollar and eighty-seven cents. And the next day would be Christmas.

2   There was clearly nothing to do but flop down on the shabby little couch and howl. So Della did it. Which instigates the moral reflection that life is made up of sobs, sniffles, and smiles, with sniffles predominating.

3   While the mistress of the home is gradually subsiding from the first stage to the second, take a look at the home. A furnished flat at $8 per week. It did not exactly beggar description, but it certainly had that word on the lookout for the mendicancy squad.

4   In the vestibule below was a letter-box into which no letter would go, and an electric button from which no mortal finger could coax a ring. Also appertaining thereunto was a card bearing the name "Mr. James Dillingham Young".

5   The "Dillingham" had been flung to the breeze during a former period of prosperity when its possessor was being paid $30 per week. Now, when the income was shrunk to $20, though, they were thinking seriously of contracting to a modest and unassuming D. But whenever Mr. James Dillingham Young came home and reached his flat above he was called "Jim" and greatly hugged by Mrs. James Dillingham Young, already introduced to you as Della. Which is all very good.

6   Della finished her cry and attended to her cheeks with the powder rag. She stood by the window and looked out dully at a gray cat walking a gray fence in a gray backyard.

7   Tomorrow would be Christmas Day, and she had only $1.87 with which to buy Jim a present. She had been saving every penny she could for months, with this result. Twenty dollars a week doesn't go far. Expenses had been greater than she had calculated. They always are. Only $1.87 to buy a present for Jim.

Extensive Reading 2

Her Jim. Many a happy hour she had spent planning for something nice for him. Something fine and rare and sterling—something just a little bit near to being worthy of the honor of being owned by Jim.

8 There was a pier-glass between the windows of the room. Perhaps you have seen a pier-glass in an $8 flat. A very thin and very agile person may, by observing his reflection in a rapid sequence of longitudinal strips, obtain a fairly accurate conception of his looks. Della, being slender, had mastered the art.

9 Suddenly she whirled from the window and stood before the glass. her eyes were shining brilliantly, but her face had lost its color within twenty seconds. Rapidly she pulled down her hair and let it fall to its full length.

10 Now, there were two possessions of the James Dillingham Youngs in which they both took a mighty pride. One was Jim's gold watch that had been his father's and his grandfather's. The other was Della's hair. Had the queen of Sheba lived in the flat across the airshaft, Della would have let her hair hang out the window some day to dry just to depreciate Her Majesty's jewels and gifts. Had King Solomon been the janitor, with all his treasures piled up in the basement, Jim would have pulled out his watch every time he passed, just to see him pluck at his beard from envy.

11 So now Della's beautiful hair fell about her rippling and shining like a cascade of brown waters. It reached below her knee and made itself almost a garment for her. And then she did it up again nervously and quickly. Once she faltered for a minute and stood still while a tear or two splashed on the worn red carpet.

12 On went her old brown jacket; on went her old brown hat. With a whirl of skirts and with the brilliant sparkle still in her eyes, she fluttered out the door and down the stairs to the street.

13 Where she stopped the sign read: "Mme. Sofronie. Hair Goods of All Kinds." One flight up Della ran, and collected herself, panting. Madame, large, too white, chilly, hardly looked the "Sofronie".

14 "Will you buy my hair?" Asked Della.

15 "I buy hair," said Madame. "Take yer hat off and let's have a sight at the looks of it."

16 Down rippled the brown cascade.

17 "Twenty dollars," said Madame, lifting the mass with a practised hand.

18 "Give it to me quick," said Della.

19 Oh, and the next two hours tripped by on rosy wings. Forget the hashed metaphor. She was ransacking the stores for Jim's present.

20 She found it at last. It surely had been made for Jim and no one else. There was no other like it in any of the stores, and she had turned all of them inside out. It was a platinum fob chain simple and chaste in design, properly proclaiming its value by substance alone and not by meretricious ornamentation—as all good things should do. It was even worthy of The Watch. As soon as she saw it she knew that it must be Jim's. It was like him. Quietness and value—the description applied to both. Twenty-one dollars they took from her for it,

and she hurried home with the 87 cents. With that chain on his watch Jim might be properly anxious about the time in any company. Grand as the watch was, he sometimes looked at it on the sly on account of the old leather strap that he used in place of a chain.

21 When Della reached home her intoxication gave way a little to prudence and reason. She got out her curling irons and lighted the gas and went to work repairing the ravages made by generosity added to love. Which is always a tremendous task, dear friends—a mammoth task.

22 Within forty minutes her head was covered with tiny, close-lying curls that made her look wonderfully like a truant schoolboy. She looked at her reflection in the mirror long, carefully, and critically.

23 "If Jim doesn't kill me," she said to herself, "before he takes a second look at me, he'll say I look like a Coney Island chorus girl. But what could I do—oh! What could I do with a dollar and eighty-seven cents?"

24 At 7 o'clock the coffee was made and the frying-pan was on the back of the stove hot and ready to cook the chops.

25 Jim was never late. Della doubled the fob chain in her hand and sat on the corner of the table near the door that he always entered. Then she heard his step on the stair away down on the first flight, and she turned white for just a moment. She had a habit for saying a little silent prayer about the simplest everyday things, and now she whispered: "Please God, make him think I am still pretty."

26 The door opened and Jim stepped in and closed it. He looked thin and very serious. Poor fellow, he was only twenty-two—and to be burdened with a family! He needed a new overcoat and he was without gloves.

27 Jim stopped inside the door, as immovable as a setter at the scent of quail. His eyes were fixed upon Della, and there was an expression in them that she could not read, and it terrified her. It was not anger, nor surprise, nor disapproval, nor horror, nor any of the sentiments that she had been prepared for. He simply stared at her fixedly with that peculiar expression on his face.

28 Della wriggled off the table and went for him.

29 "Jim, darling," she cried, "don't look at me that way. I had my hair cut off and sold because I couldn't have lived through Christmas without giving you a present. It'll grow out again—you won't mind, will you? I just had to do it. My hair grows awfully fast. Say 'Merry Christmas!' Jim, and let's be happy. You don't know what a nice— what a beautiful, nice gift I've got for you."

30 "You've cut off your hair?" Asked Jim, laboriously, as if he had not arrived at that patent fact yet even after the hardest mental labor.

31 "Cut it off and sold it," said Della. "Don't you like me just as well, anyhow? I'm me without my hair, ain't I?"

32 Jim looked about the room curiously.

33 "You say your hair is gone?" He said, with an air almost of idiocy.

Extensive Reading 2

³⁴ "You needn't look for it," said Della. "It's sold, I tell you—sold and gone, too. It's Christmas Eve, boy. Be good to me, for it went for you. Maybe the hairs of my head were numbered," she went on with sudden serious sweetness, "but nobody could ever count my love for you. Shall I put the chops on, Jim?"

³⁵ Out of his trance Jim seemed quickly to wake. He enfolded his Della. For ten seconds let us regard with discreet scrutiny some inconsequential object in the other direction. Eight dollars a week or a million a year—what is the difference? A mathematician or a wit would give you the wrong answer.

³⁵ The magi brought valuable gifts, but that was not among them. This dark assertion will be illuminated later on.

³⁶ Jim drew a package from his overcoat pocket and threw it upon the table.

³⁷ "Don't make any mistake, Dell," he said, "about me. I don't think there's anything in the way of a haircut or a shave or a shampoo that could make me like my girl any less. But if you'll unwrap that package you may see why you had me going a while at first."

³⁸ White fingers and nimble tore at the string and paper. And then an ecstatic scream of joy; and then, alas! A quick feminine change to hysterical tears and wails, necessitating the immediate employment of all the comforting powers of the lord of the flat.

³⁹ For there lay The Combs—the set of combs, side and back, that Della had worshipped long in a Broadway window. Beautiful combs, pure tortoise shell, with jewelled rims—just the shade to wear in the beautiful vanished hair. They were expensive combs, she knew, and her heart had simply craved and yearned over them without the least hope of possession. And now, they were hers, but the tresses that should have adorned the coveted adornments were gone.

⁴⁰ But she hugged them to her bosom, and at length she was able to look up with dim eyes and a smile and say: "My hair grows so fast, Jim!"

⁴¹ And then Della leaped up like a little singed cat and cried, "Oh, oh!"

⁴² Jim had not yet seen his beautiful present. She held it out to him eagerly upon her open palm. The dull precious metal seemed to flash with a reflection of her bright and ardent spirit.

⁴³ "Isn't it a dandy, Jim? I hunted all over town to find it. You'll have to look at the time a hundred times a day now. Give me your watch. I want to see how it looks on it."

⁴⁴ Instead of obeying, Jim tumbled down on the couch and put his hands under the back of his head and smiled.

⁴⁵ "Dell," said he, "let's put our Christmas presents away and keep 'em a while. They're too nice to use just at present. I sold the watch to get the money to buy your combs. And now suppose you put the chops on."

The magi, as you know, were wise men—wonderfully wise men—who brought gifts to the Babe in the manger. They invented the art of giving Christmas presents. Being wise, their gifts were no doubt wise ones, possibly bearing the privilege of exchange in case of duplication. And here I have lamely related to you the uneventful chronicle of two foolish children in a flat who most unwisely sacrificed for each other the greatest treasures of their house. But in a last word to the wise of these days let it be said that of all who give gifts these two were the wisest. O all who give and receive gifts, such as they are wisest. Everywhere they are wisest. They are the magi.

(2058 words; suggested reading time: 16 minutes)

 Reading Comprehension

Directions: *Choose the best answer from the four alternatives for the following questions.*

1. From where does Della get the $1.87, according to the text?

    A. By haggling with merchants.

    B. By shoveling sidewalks in front of stores.

    C. By stealing the money from stores.

    D. By working for the grocer, butcher, and vegetable man.

2. Why is Della upset at the beginning of the story?

    A. She lost her job shoveling in front of the stores on her block.

    B. She has been fighting with Jim.

    C. She does not have enough money to buy a nice present for Jim.

    D. She was recently arrested by the mendicancy squad.

3. What are Jim and Della's most valued possessions?

    A. Jim's watch and Della's hat.

    B. Jim's briefcase and Della's jacket.

    C. Jim's shoes and Della's cooking pot.

    D. Jim's watch and Della's hair.

4. Why does Della go to Madame Sofronie's?

    A. To look for work.

    B. To sell her hair.

    C. To beg for money.

    D. To shovel Madame Sofronie's sidewalk.

5. Which figurative language technique is used in the following sentence?

    "I couldn't have lived through Christmas without giving you a present."

    A. Metaphor

    B. Personification.

Extensive Reading 2

C. Hyperbole.

D. Understatement.

6. Which best explains why Jim is so stunned when he first sees Della?

    A. He doesn't like how his wife looks with short hair.

    B. He is shocked that she bought him such a nice gift.

    C. He doesn't recognize his wife.

    D. He bought her a gift that she can't use.

7. Which best describes the narrator's tone in this sentence from the last paragraph?

    A. Humorous.

    B. Serious.

    C. Melancholy.

    D. Intolerant.

8. With which statement would the narrator most likely agree?

    A. Jim and Della's gifts were bad because they did not consider one another's needs.

    B. Jim and Della's gifts were good because they would each get a lot of use out of their nice gifts.

    C. Jim and Della's gifts were bad because they wasted their money on things that they couldn't use.

    D. Jim and Della's gifts were good because they sacrificed so much for one another.

9. Which event happened last?

    A. Della bought Jim a gift.

    B. Della cried about only having $1.87.

    C. Della went to Madame Sofronie's.

    D. Della cut her hair.

10. Which statement best expresses the theme of this story?

    A. Make sure that you give people gifts that they can actually use.

    B. Spending time with the people you love is more important than getting them gifts.

    C. The best gifts involve sacrifice.

    D. Don't waste your money on expensive gifts.

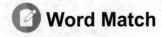
Word Match

Directions: *Match the following words with their definitions.*

1. instigate ( )	a. good judgment and caution; sensibleness
2. prosperity ( )	b. to hesitate because of being confused or not sure
3. unassuming ( )	c. a way of thinking or feeling about something
4. depreciate ( )	d. the state of being wealthy and successful
5. falter ( )	e. to purposely agitate or incite; provoke
6. prudence ( )	f. to disparage or treat as having little value; belittle
7. sentiment ( )	g. without airs or pretensions; modest; reserved
8. patent ( )	h. having or showing very strong feelings such as passion, loyalty, or desire
9. ecstatic ( )	i. readily open to notice or observation; evident; obvious
10. ardent ( )	j. in a condition of extreme delight, overpowering emotion

Extension Activity

1. Brainstorm with a partner about what features are seen in English essays.
2. O. Henry is regarded as one of the three masters of short stories in the world. Read extensively to figure out the elements of short stories and the styles of O. Henry's works.

Value Cultivation: Read and Reflect

XI SAYS

Writers and artists should produce more works that exemplify Chinese aesthetic tastes, convey modern Chinese values and notions and also reflect the common values and pursuits of all humanity.

《雨花石的等待》

Extensive Reading 2

Directions: *Translate the following paragraph into English:*

衡量一个时代的文艺成就最终要看作品，衡量文学家、艺术家的人生价值也要看作品。广大文艺工作者要精益求精、勇于创新，努力创作无愧于我们这个伟大民族、伟大时代的优秀作品。

Unit 3
Psychology

Learning Objectives

Types	Lesson A	Lesson B
Reading Skills	Denotation and Connotation	
Theme	Happiness	Seasonal Affective Disorder (SAD)
Vocabulary	Mood and Feeling	Psychology

Reading Skills

Denotation and Connotation

In linguistics, denotation and connotation are two aspects of meaning. According to Webster's *New World Dictionary*, *denotation* means the direct, explicit meaning or reference of a word or term, while *connotation* means an idea or notion suggested by or associated with a word, phrase, etc., in addition to its explicit meaning. In other words, denotation refers to the literal or primary meaning of a word, while connotation refers to the emotional or cultural associations that a word may evoke beyond its literal meaning.

Synonyms can be tricky. Sometimes, words have the same literal meaning (the word's denotation) but suggest different feelings and associations (the word's connotation). For example, if you want to compliment someone on his recent weight loss, you might say he looks thin or slender. Both thin and slender have positive connotations. You wouldn't, however, use the word scrawny as a compliment. The word scrawny has a negative connotation and implies a lack of strength.

Exercise: Choose the word or term with the most positive connotation.

1. The sales associate was very _____.

    A. assertive   B. pushy

2. We purchased some _____ furniture for the room.

    A. cheap   B. inexpensive

3. Brett told me about his _____ to increase profits.

    A. scheme   B. strategy

4. We need strong leadership from our _____.

    A. politicians   B. elected officials

5. People say that Peter has a(n) _____ management style.

   A. odd   B. strange

   C. unique   D. weird

6. Filling this position on short notice might be a(n) _____ for us.

   A. issue   B. problem

7. Luis is pretty _____. He keeps to himself and doesn't talk a whole lot.

   A. reserved   B. timid

   C. shy   D. antisocial

8. Greg is very _____. I've never seen him waste money on anything.

   A. stingy   B. cheap   C. thrifty

9. Mark tends to be a bit _____ about his work.

   A. fanatical   B. passionate   C. obsessed

10. I'm not usually so _____, but this has piqued my interest.

    A. nosy   B. curious

Lesson A

Before Reading

Warming-up Questions

1. Nowadays, emojis are widely used in emails, WeChat messages, and phone texts. Please look at the following emojis and tell us which one is your favorite. Can you describe the feelings or emotions represented by each emoji?

2. What are the possible reasons for the popularity of emojis?

Extensive Reading 2

While Reading

Write down your starting time and ending time, and then calculate your reading rate.

Starting Time: _____   Ending Time: _____

The Three Faces of Happiness

Daniel M. Haybron

1   What does happiness involve? When people think about happiness in emotional terms, they tend to picture a specific emotion: feeling happy. So powerful is this association that happiness frequently gets reduced to nothing more than cheery feelings or "smiley-face" feelings. This is a radically impoverished understanding of happiness: there's much more to being happy than just feeling happy.

2   We can usefully break happiness down into three broad dimensions. We can think of happiness as a kind of emotional evaluation of your life. At the most basic level will be responses concerning your safety and security: letting your defenses down, making yourself fully at home in your life, as opposed to taking up a defensive **stance**. I will call this state attunement with your life. Next comes responses relating to your engagement with your situation: is this worth investing much effort in your activities, or would it be wiser to withdraw or disengage from them? Finally, some emotional states serve as endorsements, signifying that your life is positively good. All three aspects of happiness are important, and different ideals of living can emphasize different parts of the picture. Americans, for instance, put more weight on endorsement or engagement states like joy and **exuberance**. Whereas Asian cultures tend to focus more on the attunement dimension.

Endorsement: Feeling Happy and Other Classic Emotions

3   Let's begin with the most familiar aspect of happiness, the endorsement dimension. The most obvious examples here are feelings of joy and sadness. It makes sense for these states to be so closely associated with happiness: they tend to accompany gains and losses, successes and failures. But it is easy to overstate their significance. Such feelings tend not to last long: you enjoy your good fortune for a bit and then get on with the business of living. Yet we should not discount the endorsement side of happiness. In general, it is far better to be cheerful than dour. Life is impoverished without regular doses of laughter. And the generic label, "feeling happy", conceals a surprising diversity of feelings. Consider the quiet joy a parent feels when looking in on his sleeping child. By contrast, the **jubilation** of a sports fan whose team has just scored a goal may be less pleasant, and less fulfilling, even if the feeling is more intense.

Engagement: Vitality and Flow

4   The second dimension of happiness concerns your engagement with your life: not bored, listless, and

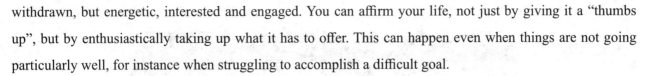

withdrawn, but energetic, interested and engaged. You can affirm your life, not just by giving it a "thumbs up", but by enthusiastically taking up what it has to offer. This can happen even when things are not going particularly well, for instance when struggling to accomplish a difficult goal.

5   There are two forms of engagement. The first of these centers on states of energy or vitality. A passionate and demanding orchestra conductor, for instance, might be exuberant, even happy. The exuberant form of happiness is typified in ideals of passionate living, notably in Nietzsche, Goethe, and countless other romantics and artists. But one need not pursue the passionate life to the Nietzschean extreme. Many people lead lives of great vitality without great suffering.

6   The second form of engagement appears more recently in the notion of *flow* developed by psychologist Mihaly Csikszentmihalyi. Flow is the state you assume when fully engaged in an activity, typically a challenging activity performed well. Athletes and musicians describe it as being "in the zone". In states of flow, you lose all senses of self-awareness, of the passage of time, and are not aware of feeling anything at all. Yet it is a highly pleasant state, and clearly a state in which you are happy. It is roughly the opposite of boredom.

Attunement: Peace of Mind, Confidence, Expansiveness

7   To understand the third dimension of happiness, consider its most familiar aspect, **tranquility**. Tranquility tends to get the back of the hand these days. People tend to crave entertainment and excitement and peace of mind can sound a lot like boredom.

8   But I would suggest that tranquility, or something like it, is the cornerstone of happiness. Perhaps it is possible to be happy without it, but the going will be tough. To see why, we need to get clearer on what tranquility is. We might think of it as "settledness": not merely peace of mind or lack of internal discord but a kind of inner surety or confidence, stability and balance.

9   Think of the state you assume when relaxing with family, or with an old and dear friend. You feel completely at home with that person. "Tranquility" seems too narrow a term for the condition of psychically being at home in one's life. I will call it a state of attunement. In this state a person relaxes and blossoms, living as seems natural to her, without inhibition. The opposite of attunement, disattunement, is not merely anxiety, but more like alienation: your circumstances are in some sense alien to you—unfamiliar, imposing, threatening. Defenses go up: anxiety, stress, insecurity. Attunement appears to have three basic aspects: inner calm (tranquility), confidence and expansiveness of mood or spirit (feeling carefree or being uncompressed).

10   One **sketch** of happiness is not yet complete. So far we've considered the felt or experienced side of happiness. But there's more to it than that.

(Excerpt from *Happiness: A Very Short Introduction*,
879 words, suggested reading time: 7 minutes)

Extensive Reading 2

Reading Comprehension

Directions: *Answer the following questions.*

1. What are the three dimensions of happiness, according to the author?
2. In the Para. 1, the author wrote, "There's much more to being happy than just feeling happy." What's the difference between "being happy" and "feeling happy"?
3. What are the features of the notion of *flow* developed by psychologist Mihaly Csikszentmihalyi?
4. Why does the author regard "tranquility" as too narrow a term for the condition of psychically being at home in one's life?
5. What are the three basic aspects of "attunement"?

Word Match

Directions: *Match the following nouns with their definitions.*

1. stance ( )	A. joyful enthusiasm
2. exuberance ( )	B. a disposition free from stress or emotion
3. jubilation ( )	C. a short report or story that gives only basic details about something
4. tranquility ( )	D. a feeling of great happiness because of a success
5. sketch ( )	E. the opinions that somebody has about something and expresses publicly

Unit 3 Psychology

After Reading

Topics for Discussion.

Have you ever experienced "flow" in your life? If yes, elaborate on the experience and share it with the rest of the class.

Lesson B

Write down your starting time and ending time, and then calculate your reading rate.

Starting Time: _____   Ending Time: _____

Tips for Dealing with Seasonal Affective Disorder

1 Seasonal changes can shift moods. In winter, they can cause irritability, fatigue, loss of concentration, weight gain and sleepiness. From December through March, River Valley Behavioral Health's call volume increases between 15 to 20 percent, said Lionel Phelps, clinical psychologist and vice president of research and development for River Valley Consulting Services.

2 "We see more people reporting depressive symptoms," he said.

3 Seasonal affective disorder (SAD) is a type of depression that sets in or starts in the winter months. Up to 6 percent of Americans experience winter depression, according to the medical journal *American Family Physician*. Another 10 to 20 percent may exhibit mild symptoms. Unlike other types of depression, it may improve as spring comes on. It is often a cyclical, recurring disorder—you'll feel depression every winter and begin to feel better each spring. Although it's less common, some people experience SAD in summer. The symptoms are less appetite, weight loss and sleeping trouble.

4 SAD depression is caused by lowered levels of serotonin, the mood-affecting brain chemical that is triggered by seasonal changes in daylight. Shorter days may also disrupt the body's biological clock—circadian rhythm—which upsets the balance of melatonin, the hormone which regulates mood and sleep patterns.

5 Seasonal affective disorder is far more common in northern climates, where days can be very short in winter. SAD affects more women than men and is likelier to occur in people under age 40 than those older than that.

Extensive Reading 2

⁶ A lack of sunshine takes a toll on many of us. Although any amount of outdoor light can help raise serotonin levels, getting light in the morning seems to offer the most benefit.

⁷ If the weather permits, take a walk. In your home or office, try sitting close to a window that faces south.

⁸ Replacing light bulbs in your home with full-spectrum light bulbs can help because they emit light similar to sunlight.

⁹ Studies have shown that upping your exercise routine can counteract SAD. Exercise raises levels of serotonin and also increases levels of endorphins, which are responsible for "runner's high" and have been shown to fight depression.

¹⁰ Moderate exercise such as walking, riding a stationary bike, or swimming is a great way to get started. But any activities that raise your heart rate, including daily chores, can help, especially if you can do them outdoors or near a sunny window. Yoga, jogging and *tai chi* can all help lift your mood.

¹¹ Vitamin D is necessary for the synthesis of serotonin and dopamine (chemicals associated with depression), so researchers concluded that a link between low vitamin D levels and depression was logical. The Vitamin D Council recommends 2,000 IU daily, but suggests taking more if you get little exposure to the sun.

¹² Eat more fish. Fatty fish, such as salmon and sardines, contain omega-3 fatty acids. Studies have found that people who have low levels of two chemicals found in fish, eicosapentaenoic acid (EPA) and docosahexaenoic acid (DHA), are at increased risk for depression. Either eat more fish—at least three times a week—or take fish oil capsules to combat SAD.

¹³ Year-end panic refers to the self-reproach and overall feeling of panic brought about by the approach of the year's end, often due to a poor financial year and pressure from work and family.

¹⁴ Psychological experts suggest that we should avoid peer competition. While regretting for the failed plans in the past year, you can still make resolution to do it better in the coming year.

¹⁵ "It's normal to have some days when you feel down," according to information found on the Mayo Clinic website. "But if you feel down for days at a time and you can't get motivated to do activities you normally enjoy, see your doctor."

(624 words, suggested reading time: 5 minutes)

Reading Comprehension

Directions: *Choose the best answer from the four alternatives for the following questions.*

1. Who among the four is most likely to suffer from SAD?

   A. A young man at the age of 25.

B. A young woman at the age of 30.

C. An older man at the age of 65.

D. An older woman at the age of 65.

2. Which one is not a symptom of Summer SAD?

    A. Loss of appetite.   B. Weight gain.

    C. Weight loss.   D. Sleeping troubles.

3. What is the meaning of "take a toll on"?

    A. Benefit.   B. Do harm to.   C. Affect.   D. Help.

4. What is the meaning of "runner's high"?

    A. The runner's high speed.

    B. The runner's high fever.

    C. The runner's excitement.

    D. The runner's high frequency.

5. Which one of the following is not a possible reason for SAD?

    A. Seasonal changes.

    B. Year-end panic.

    C. Low vitamin D level.

    D. The balance of melatonin.

✎ Word Formation

***Directions**: Fill in each of the blanks with the given word in its proper form.*

1. Overwork, weather changes, and _____ are important factors that lead to stroke. (irritable)

Extensive Reading 2

2. She suffered from severe _____ after losing her job. (depressed)
3. Graduates have to fight for jobs in a highly _____ market. (competition)
4. He called on the authorities to stop public _____. (order)
5. I'm not _____ allowed to stay out late. (normal)

 **Extension Activity**

Directions: *Have you ever personally experienced winter SAD or summer SAD? If yes, what were your symptoms? Are they the same as listed in the picture?*

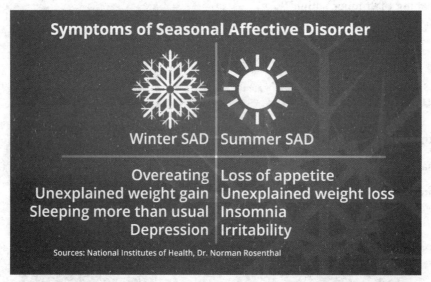

Value Cultivation: Read and Reflect

How Is Mental Health Relevant to Me?

October 10th is World Mental Health Day, which was initiated by WHO in 1992 to raise public awareness of mental health around the world.

Mental health includes our emotional, psychological, and social well-being.

❖ It affects how we think, feel, and act.

❖ It determines how we handle stress, relate to others, and make choices.

❖ Mental health is important at every stage of life, from childhood and adolescence through adulthood.

❖ Some typical potential early warning signs:

1 in 5 adults
experience mental illness each year *

39% of college students
experence a serious mental health issue †

⟶ **2/3 of students** ⟵
with anxiety or depression don't seek treatment †

- Pulling away from people and usual activities.
- Having low or no energy; having trouble performing daily tasks.
- Smoking, drinking, or using drugs more than usual.
- Feeling unusually confused, forgetful, on edge, angry, upset, worried, or scared.
- Eating or sleeping too much or too little.
- Neglecting personal hygiene.
- Thinking of harming oneself or others.

If you find yourself or someone you know has been struggling with some of these symptoms for a significant length of time (persisting past 1-2 weeks), it might be a good idea to talk to someone about it.

Unit 4

Science

Learning Objectives

Types	Lesson A	Lesson B
Reading Skills	Sentence Understanding	
Theme	Definition of Science	Astronomy Apps
Vocabulary	Science	Astronomy

Reading Skills

Sentence Understanding

In English, we have simple sentences, compound sentences, and complex sentences. All of these can be extended into long sentences that become a barrier for you to understand the article containing them. In some cases, you can hardly figure out their meanings even though you know every word in those sentences.

Simple Sentences

To understand long sentences in reading, you must know different types of English sentence structures. The first we'll consider is the simple sentence. No matter how long the sentence is, a simple sentence has only one clause. What you need to do is to identify the basic elements of the sentence. In other words, you must find the subject, predicate, and object.

Example:

The tall, good-looking boy with the curly blond hair over there laughed uproariously at his best friend's suggestion.

The subject is *the boy*. The predicate is *laugh at*. The object is *the suggestion*. Therefore, the key information in this sentence is, "The boy laughed at the suggestion."

Compound Sentences

The second structure is the compound sentence. To be a compound sentence, it needs at least two subjects and two predicates. If both independent clauses use the same subject, it must be stated twice, as in the quote below, for the sentence to be compound.

Example:

I alone cannot change the world, but I can cast a stone across the water to create many ripples.

The two clauses in this compound sentence have independent subjects and predicates:

In the first clause, the subject is "I" and the predicate is "cannot change the world" . In the second clause, the same subject "I" is restated and the predicate is "cast a stone".

Complex Sentences

Another sentence structure is the complex sentence. Complex sentences always have a main clause and at least one subordinate clause. The clauses are linked by subordinating conjunctions such as *although*, *because*, *when*, *while*, and *who*.

Example:

The prevailing notion that wind power is too costly results largely from early research which focused on turbines with huge blades that stood hundreds of meters tall.

The main clause here is, "The prevailing notion results largely from early research". This sentence includes three subordinate clauses.

The first one (that wind power is too costly) explains the details of the notion.

The second one (focusing on turbines with huge blades) describes the content of the research.

The last one (specifying hundreds of meters tall) describes the size of the blade.

For longer complex sentences, you need to tell which is the main clause and which are the subordinate clauses.

Compound-complex Sentences

A compound-complex sentence consists of at least two independent clauses and at least one dependent clause.

Example:

If you will let me, I would like to show you how sentences are formed and teach you to master the English language.

You can tell that it's a compound-complex sentence by getting rid of the conjunctions and looking at each clause. If there are at least two independent clauses and one dependent clause, then it's a compound-complex sentence.

Exercises: Analyze the structure of each sentence below.

1. To land her dream job after college, Sally maintained good academic standing through her four years at the college, gained crucial skills required at the workplace, networked in the company, and prepared like hell for the recruitment process.
2. Totally without light and subjected to intense pressures hundreds of times greater than at the Earth's surface, the deep-ocean bottom is a hostile environment to humans, in some ways as forbidding and remote as the void of outer space.
3. Confident people are not negatively influenced by criticism because they do not think that criticism of them means a denial of their significance.
4. His blue eyes were light, bright, and sparkling behind half-moon spectacles, and his nose was very long and crooked, as though it had been broken at least twice.

Extensive Reading 2

Lesson A

Before Reading

Brainstorming

Directions: *The word "science" probably brings to mind many different pictures: a thick textbook, white lab coats and microscopes, an astronomer peering through a telescope, a naturalist in the rainforest, Einstein's equations scribbled on a chalkboard, the launch of the space shuttle, bubbling beaker... Can you add more examples to this list?*

While Reading

Write down your starting time and ending time, and then calculate your reading rate.

Starting Time: _____   Ending Time: _____

What Is Science?

Ira Remsen[1]

1   First, then, what is science? Surely there can be no difficulty in answering this, and yet I fear that, if I should pass through this or any other audience with the question, I should get many different answers.

2   A certain lady, whom I know better than any other, has told me that, should she ever be permitted to

---

[1] Ira Remsen (1846-1927), American chemist and educator and professor of chemistry in John Hopkins University, 1876-1913; president of the same university, 1901-1912. Discoverer of saccharine; founder of the *American Chemical Journal*.

marry a second time, she would not marry a scientific man, because scientific men are so terribly accurate. I often hear the same general idea expressed, and it is clear that accuracy is one **attribute** of science according to **prevailing** opinions. But accuracy alone is not science. When we hear a game of baseball or of whist spoken of as thoroughly scientific, I suppose the idea here, too, is that the games are played accurately; that is, to use the technical expression, without errors.

3   Again, there are those who seem to think that science is something that has been devised by the Evil One for the purpose of undermining religion. The idea is not so common as it was a few years ago, when the professors of scientific subjects in our colleges were generally objects of suspicion. The change which has come over the world in this respect within my own memory is simply **astounding**. In general terms, an agreement has been reached between those who represent religion and those who represent science. This agreement is certainly not final, but it gives us a modus vivendi, and the clash of arms is now rarely heard. Religion now takes into consideration the claims of science, and science recognizes the great fundamental truths of religion. Each should strengthen the other, and in time, no doubt, each will strengthen the other.

4   Probably the idea most commonly held in regard to science is that it is something that gives us a great many useful inventions. The steam engine, the telegraph, the telephone, the trolley car, dyestuffs, medicines, explosives—these are the fruits of science, and without these science is of no **avail**. I propose farther on to discuss this subject more fully than I can at this stage of my remarks, so that I may pass over it lightly here. I need only say now that useful inventions are not a necessary consequence of scientific work, and that scientific work does not depend upon useful applications for its value. These **propositions**, which are familiar enough to scientific men, are apt to surprise those who are outside of scientific circles. I hope before I get through to show you that the propositions are true.

5   Science, then, is not simply accuracy, although it would be worthless if it were not accurate; it is not devised for the purpose of undermining religion; and its object is not the making of useful inventions. Then what is it?

6   One dictionary gives this definition: "Knowledge; knowledge of principles and causes, **ascertained** truths or facts… Accumulated and established knowledge which has been **systematized** and formulated with reference to the discovery of general truths or the operation of general laws, … especially such knowledge when it relates to the physical world, and its phenomena, the nature, constitution, and forces of nature, the qualities and functions of living tissues, etc."

7   One writer says: "The **distinction** between science and art is that science is a body of principles and **deductions** to explain the nature of some matter. An art is a body of precepts with practical skill for the completion of some work. A science teaches us to know; an art, to do. In art, truth is means to an end; in science, it is the only end. Hence the practical arts are not to be classed among the sciences." Another writer

Extensive Reading 2

says, "Science and art may be said to be investigations of truth; but one, science, inquires for the sake of knowledge; the other, art, for the sake of production; and hence science is more concerned with higher truths, art with the lower; and science never is engaged, as art, is, in productive application."

8   Science, then, has for its object the accumulation and systematization of knowledge, the discovery of truth. The astronomer is trying to learn more and more about the celestial bodies, their motions, their composition, their changes. Through his labors, carried on for many centuries, we have the science of astronomy. The geologist has, on the other hand, confined his attention to the earth, and he is trying to learn as much as possible of its composition and structure, and of the processes that have been operating through untold ages to give us the earth as it now is. He has given us the science of geology, which consists of a vast mass of knowledge carefully systematized and of **innumerable** deductions of interest and value. If the time shall ever come when, through the labor of the geologist, all that can possibly be learned in regard to the structure and development of the earth shall have been learned, the occupation of the geologist would be gone. But that time will never come.

9   And so I might go on pointing out the general character of the work done by different classes of scientific men, but this would be tedious. We should only have brought home to us in each case the fact that, no matter what the science may be with which we are dealing, its disciples are simply trying to learn all they can in the field in which they are working. As I began with a reference to astronomy, let me close with a reference to chemistry. Astronomy has to deal with the largest bodies and the greatest distances of the universe; chemistry, on the other hand, has to deal with the smallest particles and the shortest distances of the universe. Astronomy is the science of the infinitely great; chemistry is the science of the infinitely little. The chemist wants to know what things are made of and, in order to find this out, he has to push his work to the smallest particles of matter. Then he comes face to face with facts that lead him to the belief that the smallest particles he can weigh by the aid of the most delicate balance, and the smallest particles he can see with the aid of the most powerful microscope, are immense as compared with those of which he has good reason to believe the various kinds of matter to be made up. It is for this reason that I say that chemistry is the science of the infinitely little.

10 Thus I have tried to show what science is and what it is not.

(*Science Magazine*, 1929, pp. 229-232

1104 words; suggested reading time: 9 minutes)

Reading Comprehension

Directions: *Answer the following questions.*

1. What can we learn from Para. 1?

2. Why does the author employ the example of baseball in Para. 2?

3. Paraphrase the sentence, "I need only say now that useful inventions are not a necessary consequence of scientific work and that scientific work does not depend upon useful applications for its value."

4. What is the function of Para. 5?

5. Summarize the different definitions of science presented in this article.

6. According to this article, how is a science different from an art?

7. What does the word "systematization" in Para. 8 mean?

8. Do you agree with the writer's definition of science? Why or why not?

Word Match

Directions: *Match the following words with their definitions.*

Group 1: Adjectives

1. prevailing ( )	A. discovered or determined by scientific observation
2. astounding ( )	B. organized
3. ascertained ( )	C. so surprisingly impressive as to stun or overwhelm
4. systematized ( )	D. too numerous to be counted
5. innumerable ( )	E. most frequent or common; encountered generally, especially at the present time

Group 2: Nouns

1. attribute ( )	A. something that is inferred (deduced or entailed or implied)
2. avail ( )	B. a statement or an idea that people can consider or discuss to decide whether it is true
3. proposition ( )	C. a discrimination between things as different
4. distinction ( )	D. an abstraction belonging to or characteristic of an entity
5. deduction ( )	E. a means of serving

 Cloze

Directions: *Fill in each blank with the proper form of one of the words given below.*

based	systematic	cultural	entails	inorganic
biological	behavior	fundamental	concerned	pursuit

 A science is any system of knowledge that is ___1___ with the physical world and its phenomena and that ___2___ unbiased observations and ___3___ experimentation. In general, a science involves

Extensive Reading 2

a __4__ of knowledge covering general truths or the operations of __5__ laws. Science can be divided into different branches __6__ on the subject of study. The physical sciences study the __7__ world and comprise the fields of astronomy, physics, chemistry, and the Earth sciences. The __8__ sciences, such as biology and medicine, study the organic world of life and its processes. Social sciences like anthropology and economics study the social and __9__ aspects of human __10__.

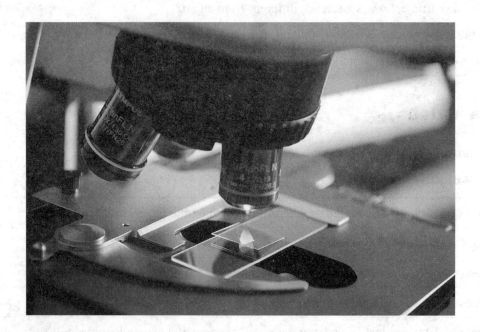

After Reading

Topics for Discussion.

1. Does science play a crucial role in your daily life and study? Please illustrate with examples.
2. Some people hold the opinion that the sciences and the humanities are fundamentally in opposition. What's your opinion?

Lesson B

Write down your starting time and ending time, and then calculate your reading rate.

Starting Time: _____   Ending Time: _____

The Best Astronomy Apps for Smartphones, Tablets, and Computers

Carolyn Collins Petersen[①]

1   In the old days of stargazing, before smartphones and tablets and desktop computers existed, astronomers relied on star charts and catalogs to find things in the sky. Of course, they also had to guide their own telescopes and, in some cases, rely simply on the naked eye for observing the night sky. With the digital revolution, tools that people use for navigation, communication, and education are prime targets for astronomy apps and programs. These come in handy in addition to astronomy books and other products.

2   There are dozens of decent apps for astronomy out there, as well as apps from most of the major space missions. Each one delivers up-to-date content for people interested in various missions. Whether someone is a stargazer or simply interested in what's going on "up there", these digital assistants open up the cosmos for individual exploration.

3   Many of these apps and programs are free or have in-app purchases to help users customize their experience. In all cases, these programs offer access to cosmic information early astronomers could only dream of accessing. For mobile device users, apps offer great portability, allowing users access to electronic stars in the field.

How Digital Astronomy Assistants Work

4   Mobile and desktop stargazing applications have as their main purpose to show observers the night sky at a given location on Earth. Since computers and mobiles have access to time, date, and location information (often through GPS), the programs and apps know where they are, and in the case of an app on a smartphone, uses the device's compass to know where it's pointed. Using databases of stars, planets, and deep-sky objects, plus some chart-creation code, these programs can deliver an accurate digital chart. All the user has to do is look at the chart to know what is up in the sky.

5   Digital star charts show an object's position, but also deliver information about the object itself (its magnitude, its type, and distance). Some programs can also tell a star's classification (that is, what type of star it is), and can animate the apparent motion of planets, the Sun, Moon, comets, and asteroids across the sky over time.

Recommended Astronomy Apps

6   A quick search of app sites reveals a wealth of astronomy apps that work well on smartphones and tablets. There are also many programs that make themselves at home on desktop and laptop computers. Many of these products can also be used to control a telescope, making them doubly useful for sky observers. Nearly all the apps and programs are fairly easy for beginners to pick up and allow people to learn astronomy

---

① Petersen, Carolyn Collins. "The Best Astronomy Apps for Smartphones, Tablets, and Computers." ThoughtCo.com

Extensive Reading 2

at their own pace.

7   Apps such as StarMap 2 have substantial resources available for stargazers, even in the free edition. Customizations include adding new databases, telescope controls, and a unique series of tutorials for beginners. It is available to users with iOS devices.

8   Another one, called Sky Map, is a favorite among Android users and is free of charge. Described as a "hand-held planetarium for your device" it helps users identify stars, planets, nebulae, and more.

9   There are also apps available for the tech-enabled younger users that allow them to explore the sky at their own pace. The Night Sky is aimed at kids eight years and older and packed with many of the same databases as the higher-end or more complex apps. It's available for iOS devices.

10   Starwalk has two versions of its popular astro-app, one aimed directly at kids. It's called "Star Walk Kids", and is available for both iOS and Android devices. For the adults, the company also has a satellite tracker app as well as a solar system exploration product.

Best Space Agency Apps

11   Of course, there are more than stars, planets, and galaxies out there. Stargazers quickly become acquainted with other sky objects, such as satellites. Knowing when the International Space Station is due to pass overhead affords an observer a chance to plan ahead to catch a glimpse. That's where the NASA app comes in handy. Available on a wide variety of platforms, it showcases NASA content and supplies satellite tracking, content, and more. The European Space Agency (ESA) has devised similar apps, as well.

The Best Programs for Desktop Astronomers

12   Not to be outdone, developers have created many programs for desktop and laptop applications. These can be as simple as star chart printing or as complex as using the program and computer to run a home observatory. One of the best-known and completely free programs out there is Stellarium. It's totally open source and is easy to update with free databases and other enhancements. Many observers use Cartes du Ciel, a chart-making program that is also free to download and use.

13   Some of the most powerful and up-to-date programs are not free but are definitely worth checking out, especially by users interested in using the apps and programs to control their observatories. These include TheSky, which can be used as a stand-alone charting program, or a controller for a pro-grade mount. Another is called StarryNight. It comes in several flavors, including one with telescope control and another for beginners and classroom study.

Browsing the Universe

14   Browser-based pages also afford fascinating access to the sky. Sky-Map, offers users a chance to explore the universe easily and imaginatively. Google Earth also has a product that's free, called Google Sky that does the same thing, with the ease of navigation that Google Earth users are familiar with.

Unit 4 Science

(https://www.thoughtco.com/best-astronomy-apps-4160999,
924 words; suggested reading time: 8 minutes)

Reading Comprehension

Directions: *Answer the following questions.*

1. What is the main idea of this article?
2. How did astronomers observe the sky before the existence of smartphones, tablets, and laptops?
3. Are all the apps and programs mentioned free of charge?
4. How can these programs deliver an accurate digital chart?
5. Are the apps and programs accessible for beginners?
6. What can the NASA app showcase?
7. List the advantages of Stellarium.
8. What are the best programs for Desktop users according to the recommendations in this article?

Word Formation

Directions: *Fill in each of the blanks with the given word in its proper form.*

1. It's hoped that the _____ will enable scientists to see deeper into the universe than ever before. (scope)
2. Pack ice around Iceland was becoming a threat to _____. (navigate)
3. Consumers are becoming more worried about giving personal information to tech companies to get _____ products and services. (customize)
4. I bought it for its _____, not its appearance. (portable)
5. Living in a flourishing city, you can also see an actual beautiful _____ sky. (star)
6. Its tariffs cater for four basic _____ of customer. (classify)
7. _____ numbers of people support the reforms. (substance)
8. Employees should be fully _____ with emergency procedures. (acquaint)
9. The result will _____ turn out to be just the opposite of their wish. (definite)
10. The hotel is decorated _____ and attractively. (imagine)

Extension Activity

Directions: *How have smartphone applications affected your life? Write a paragraph on the pros and cons of using them.*

Extensive Reading 2

Value Cultivation: Read and Reflect

Directions: *Read and translate the following paragraph into Chinese.*

President Xi Jinping on Friday called for the accelerated transformation of China into a scientific and technological powerhouse, and for it to achieve higher levels of self-reliance and strength in science and technology to provide strategic support for national development. Xi made the remarks when addressing the 20th General Assembly of Academicians from the Chinese Academy of Sciences, the 15th General Assembly of Academicians from the Chinese Academy of Engineering, and the 10th National Congress of the China Association for Science and Technology.

Unit 5

Language

Learning Objectives

Types	Lesson A	Lesson B
Reading Skills	Fact and Opinion	
Theme	Linguistic Data	Being Bilingual
Vocabulary	Linguistics	Language Learning

Extensive Reading 2

Reading Skills

Fact and Opinion

Most reading passages contain ideas based on facts and opinions; therefore, the ability to distinguish between facts and opinions is of great significance, because it can help us achieve a deeper level of understanding in our reading.

Facts are statements that tell what really happened or what really the case is. A fact can be proved or disproved with direct evidence. It is something known by actual experience or observation. Therefore, it is inarguable, and can not be discussed.

Opinions are statements of belief, judgment, or feeling about a subject. Opinions, of course, are often based on facts, but they also involve the writer's interpretation or opinion, with which you can agree or disagree. Look at the following example:

In America, the FBI reports that cyber-crime is rising, costing individuals and businesses billions of dollars. And the war on this kind of crime seems hard to win.

In the above paragraph, the first sentence is a fact, for it is based on the FBI's report, while the second sentence is the author's opinion.

But sometimes, facts and opinions may be mixed together, making it hard for the reader to dissociate one from the other. Very often, opinion is presented as if it were a fact.

Consequently, readers should be always alert to the opinion clue words that appear in the passage. Some words can serve as clues to statements of some kind of opinion. For example, *probably, perhaps, possible, usually, often, sometimes,* and *on occasion* are used to limit a statement of opinion and to indicate the possibility of other opinions. Other words, such as *I believe, I think, in my opinion, I feel,* and *I suggest,* say clearly that an opinion will follow.

Exercise: Read the following sentences, and decide which are facts and which are opinions. Indicate your choice by writing F for Fact or O for Opinion in the boxes provided.

☐ 1. The best advice to follow when choosing a career is to choose the one that promises the highest income.

☐ 2. The sun rises in the east and sets in the west.

☐ 3. Most people look forward to summer because there are so many more fun activities available than during the winter.

☐ 4. Current best-selling novels are far superior to the best-sellers of past years and cover a much wider range of interests.

☐ 5. Mount McKinley in Alaska, at an impressive height of over 20,000 feet, is the highest mountain in North America.

☐ 6. Alcoholism, the uncontrollable need for alcohol, is a serious disease that affects millions of people in our country.

☐ 7. With all its vibrant colors, pleasant weather, and fun festivals, fall is the most favored of the four seasons.

☐ 8. Light travels faster than sound.

☐ 9. All intelligent people recognize the need for a college education.

☐ 10. George Washington was inaugurated as the first president of the United States on April 30, 1789.

Before Reading

Warming-up Questions

1. Besides English, have you ever learned any other foreign language? If yes, what is it? How long have you learned it? Do you like it?
2. Can you think of any benefit of being bilingual or multilingual?

Extensive Reading 2

While Reading

Write down your starting time and ending time, and then calculate your reading rate.

Starting Time: _____   Ending Time: _____

Obtaining Linguistic Data

1   Many procedures are available for obtaining data about a language. They range from a carefully planned, intensive field investigation in a foreign country to a casual **introspection** about one's mother tongue carried out in an armchair at home.

2   In all cases, someone has to act as a source of language data—an informant. Informants are (ideally) native speakers of a language, who provide utterances for analysis and other kinds of information about the language (e.g. translations, comments about correctness, or judgments on usage). Often, when studying their mother tongue, linguists act as their own informants, judging the **ambiguity**, acceptability, or other properties of utterances against their own intuitions. Convenience of this approach makes it widely used, and it is considered the norm in the generative approach to linguistics. But a linguist's personal judgments are often uncertain, or disagree with the judgments of other linguists, at which point recourse is needed to more objective methods of enquiry, using non-linguists as informants. The latter procedure is unavoidable when working on foreign languages, or child speech.

3   Many factors must be considered when selecting informants—whether one is working with single speakers (a common situation when languages have not been described before), two people interacting, small groups or large-scale samples. Age, sex, social background and other aspects of identity are important, as these factors are known to influence the kind of language used. The topic of conversation and the characteristics of the social setting (e.g. the level of formality) are also highly relevant, as are the personal

qualities of the informants (e.g. their fluency and **consistency**). For larger studies, scrupulous attention has been paid to the sampling theory employed, and in all cases, decisions have to be made about the best investigative techniques to use.

4   Today, researchers often tape-record informants. This enables the linguist's claims about the language to be checked, and provides a way of making those claims more accurate ("difficult" pieces of speech can be listened to repeatedly). But obtaining naturalistic, good-quality data is never easy. People talk abnormally when they know they are being recorded, and sound quality can be poor. A variety of tape-recording procedures have thus been devised to **minimize** the "observer's **paradox**" (how to observe the way people behave when they are not being observed). Some recordings are made without the speakers being aware of the fact—a procedure that obtains very natural data, though ethical objections must be anticipated.

5   Alternatively, attempts can be made to make the speaker forget about the recording, such as keeping the tape recorder out of sight, or using radio microphones. A useful technique is to introduce a topic that quickly involves the speaker, and **stimulates** a natural language style (e.g. asking older informants about how times have changed in their locality).

6   An audio tape recording does not solve all the linguist's problems, however. Speech is often unclear and ambiguous. Where possible, therefore, the recording has to be **supplemented** by the observer's written comments on the non-verbal behavior of the participants, and about the context in general. A facial expression, for example, can dramatically **alter** the meaning of what is said. Video recordings avoid these problems to a large extent, but even they have limitations (the camera cannot be everywhere), and transcriptions always benefit from any additional commentary provided by an observer.

7   Linguists also make great use of structured sessions, in which they systematically ask their informants for utterances that describe certain actions, objects or behavior. With a bilingual informant, or through the use of an interpreter, it is possible to use translation techniques ("How do you say table in your language?"). A large number of points can be covered in a short time, using interview worksheets and questionnaires. Often, the researcher wishes to obtain information about just a single variable, in which case a restricted set of questions may be used: a particular feature of pronunciation, for example, can be **elicited** by asking the informant to say a restricted set of words. There are also several direct methods of elicitation, such as asking informants to fill in the blanks in a substitution frame (e.g. I ____ see a car), or feeding them the wrong stimulus for correction ("Is it possible to say I no can see?").

8   A representative sample of language, compiled for the purpose of linguistic analysis, is known as a corpus. A corpus enables the linguist to make unbiased statements about frequency of usage, and it provides accessible data for the use of different researchers. Its range and size are variable. Some corpora attempt to cover the language as a whole, taking extracts from many kinds of text; others are extremely selective,

Extensive Reading 2

providing a collection of material that deals only with a particular linguistic feature. The size of the corpus depends on practical factors, such as the time available to collect, process and store the data: it can take up to several hours to provide an accurate transcription of a few minutes of speech. Sometimes a small sample of data will be enough to decide a linguistic **hypothesis**; by contrast, corpora in major research projects can total millions of words. An important principle is that all corpora, whatever their size, are inevitably limited in their coverage, and always need to be supplemented by data derived from the intuitions of native speakers of the language, through either introspection or experimentation.

(from *Cambridge English IELTS Book 4*; 882 words; suggested reading time: 7 minutes)

 Reading Comprehension

Part 1 Match the paragraph.

Directions: *The passage has seven paragraphs labeled 1-7. Which paragraph contains the following information? Write the correct number in the boxes below. You may use any number more than once.*

☐ 1. the effect of recording on the way people talk

☐ 2. the importance of taking notes on body language

☐ 3. the fact that language is influenced by social situation

☐ 4. how informants can be helped to be less self-conscious

☐ 5. various methods that can be used to generate specific data

Part 2 Complete the table below.

Directions: *Choose NO MORE THAN THREE WORDS from the passage for each answer.*

Methods of Obtaining Linguistic Data	Advantages	Disadvantages
_____ as informant	convenient	method of enquiry not objective enough
non-linguist as informant	necessary with _____ and child speech	the number of factors to be considered
recording an informant	allows linguists' claims to be checked	_____ of sound
videoing an informant	allows speakers' _____ to be observed	_____ might miss certain things

Part 3 Complete the summary of Para. 7 below.

Directions: *Choose NO MORE THAN THREE WORDS from the passage for each answer.*

A linguist can use a corpus to comment objectively on _____. Some corpora include a wide range of language while others are used to focus on a _____. The length of time the process takes will affect the _____ of the corpus. No corpus can ever cover the whole language and so linguists often find themselves relying on the additional information that can be gained from the _____ of those who speak the language concerned.

Word Match

Group 1: Nouns

1. introspection ( )	A. a tentative theory about the natural world; a concept that is not yet verified but that if true would explain certain facts or phenomena
2. ambiguity ( )	B. logical coherence and accordance with the facts
3. paradox ( )	C. the contemplation of your own thoughts and desires and conduct
4. consistency ( )	D. an expression whose meaning cannot be determined from its context
5. hypothesis ( )	E. (logic) a statement that contradicts itself

Group 2: Verbs

1. minimize ( )	A. to call forth (emotions, feelings, and responses)
2. stimulate ( )	B. to make small or insignificant
3. supplement ( )	C. to cause to change; make different; cause a transformation
4. alter ( )	D. cause to do; cause to act in a specified manner
5. elicit ( )	E. add as a supplement to what seems insufficient

After Reading

Directions: *Here is a survey for you as language learners to better understand the challenges and preferences of language learning.*

Section 1: Learning Preferences

1. What is your primary reason for learning English?

   -Education   -Work   -Travel   -Personal interest

   -Other (please specify)

2. Which of the following English skills do you focus on the most? (Select all that apply)

   -Listening   -Speaking   -Reading

   -Writing   -Grammar   -Vocabulary

3. How do you usually learn English? (Select all that apply)

   -Formal classroom setting   -Online courses   -Mobile apps

   -Self-study with books/materials   -Conversational practice

   -Other (please specify)

4. How many hours per week do you spend learning English?

Extensive Reading 2

Section 2: Challenges and Motivation

5. What do you find most challenging about learning English?

   -Pronunciation   -Grammar rules   -Vocabulary

   -Listening comprehension   -Speaking confidence   -Other (please specify)

6. How do you stay motivated to learn English?

   -Setting goals   -Tracking progress   -Rewards for achievements

   -Support from teachers/peers   -Other (please specify)

Section 3: Learning Strategies

7. Which of the following learning strategies do you frequently use? (Select all that apply)

   -Repetition and memorization

   -Using flashcards   -Keeping a language journal

   -Engaging in conversations with native speakers

   -Watching movies or TV shows in English

   -Listening to English music   -Reading English books or articles

   -Taking notes in English   -Using language learning software or apps

   -None of these   -Other (please specify)

8. How often do you review and practice what you have learned?

   -Daily   -A few times a week   -Once a week

   -Occasionally   -Rarely

9. Do you set specific learning goals for yourself? If yes, please describe one of your recent goals.

10. How do you measure your progress in learning English?

    -Self-assessment   -Formal assessments (e.g., tests, exams)

    -Feedback from teachers or peers   -Other (please specify)

11. Have you ever used a language learning strategy that was particularly effective for you? If so, please describe it and explain why it was effective.

12. Are there any learning strategies that you have tried but found to be ineffective? If so, please explain why.

13. How important is it for you to understand the cultural context when learning English?

    -Very important   -Somewhat important

    -Not very important   -Not important at all

Section 4: Resources and Feedback

14. Which resources have been most helpful for your English learning? (Select all that apply)

    -Textbooks   -Online videos (e.g., YouTube)

    -Podcasts   -Language exchange programs

Unit 5 Language

-Social media   -Other (please specify)

15. What additional resources or support would you like to have to improve your English?

16. Do you have any other comments or suggestions regarding English language learning?

Lesson B

Write down your starting time and ending time, and then calculate your reading rate.

Starting Time: _____   Ending Time: _____

The Benefits of Being Bilingual

1 According to the latest figures, the majority of the world's population is now bilingual or multilingual, having grown up speaking two or more languages. In the past, such children were considered to be at a disadvantage compared with their monolingual peers. Over the past few decades, however, technological advances have allowed researchers to look more deeply at how bilingualism interacts with and changes the cognitive and neurological systems, thereby identifying several clear benefits of being bilingual.

2 Research shows that when a bilingual person uses one language, the other is active at the same time. When we hear a word, we don't hear the entire word all at once: the sounds arrive in sequential order. Long before the word is finished, the brain's language system begins to guess what that word might be. If you hear "can", you will likely activate words like "candy" and "candle" as well, at least during the earlier stages of word recognition. For bilingual people, this activation is not limited to a single language; auditory input activates corresponding words regardless of the language to which they belong. Some of the most compelling

evidence for this phenomenon, called "language co-activation", comes from studying eye movements. A Russian-English bilingual asked to "pick up a marker" from a set of objects would look more at a stamp than someone who doesn't know Russian, because the Russian word for "stamp", *marka*, sounds like the English word he or she heard, "marker". In cases like this, language co-activation occurs because what the listener hears could map onto words in either language.

³ Having to deal with this persistent linguistic competition can result in difficulties, however. For instance, knowing more than one language can cause speakers to name pictures more slowly, and can increase "tip-of-the-tongue states", when you can almost, but not quite, bring a word to mind. As a result, the constant juggling of two languages creates a need to control how much a person accesses a language at any given time. For this reason, bilingual people often perform better on tasks that require conflict management. In the classic Stroop Task, people see a word and are asked to name the color of the word's font. When the colour and the Word Match (i.e., the word "red" printed in red), people correctly name the color more quickly than when the colour and the word don't match (i.e., the word "red" printed in blue). This occurs because the word itself ("red") and its font color (blue) conflict. Bilingual people often excel at tasks such as this, which tap into the ability to ignore competing perceptual information and focus on the relevant aspects of the input. Bilinguals are also better at switching between two tasks; for example, when bilinguals have to switch from categorizing objects by color (red or green) to categorizing them by shape (circle or triangle), they do so more quickly than monolingual people, reflecting better cognitive control when having to make rapid changes of strategy.

⁴ It also seems that the neurological roots of the bilingual advantage extend to brain areas more traditionally associated with sensory processing. When monolingual and bilingual adolescents listen to simple speech sounds without any intervening background noise, they show highly similar brain stem responses. When researchers play the same sound to both groups in the presence of background noise, however, the bilingual listeners' neural response is considerably larger, reflecting better encoding of the sound's fundamental frequency, a feature of sound closely related to pitch perception.

⁵ Such improvements in cognitive and sensory processing may help a bilingual person to process information in the environment, and help explain why bilingual adults acquire a third language better than monolingual adults master a second language. This advantage may be rooted in the skill of focusing on information about the new language while reducing interference from the languages they already know.

⁵ Research also indicates that bilingual experience may help to keep the cognitive mechanisms sharp by recruiting alternate brain networks to compensate for those that become damaged during aging. Older bilinguals enjoy improved memory relative to monolingual people, which can lead to real-world health benefits. In a study of over 200 patients with Alzheimer's disease, a degenerative brain disease, bilingual

patients reported showing initial symptoms of the disease an average of five years later than monolingual patients. In a follow-up study, researchers compared the brains of bilingual and monolingual patients matched on the severity of Alzheimer's symptoms. Surprisingly, the bilinguals' brains had more physical signs of disease than their monolingual counterparts, even though their outward behavior and abilities were the same. If the brain is an engine, bilingualism may help it to go farther on the same amount of fuel.

6   Furthermore, the benefits associated with bilingual experience seem to start very early. In one study, researchers taught seven-month-old babies growing up in monolingual or bilingual homes that when they heard a tinkling sound, a puppet appeared on one side of a screen. Halfway through the study, the puppet began appearing on the opposite side of the screen. In order to get a reward, the infants had to adjust the rule they'd learned; only the bilingual babies were able to successfully learn the new rule. This suggests that for very young children, as well as for older people, navigating a multilingual environment imparts advantages that transfer far beyond language.

(*Cambridge English IELTS Book 12*; 884 words; suggested reading time: 7 minutes)

Reading Comprehension

Part 1 Do the following statements agree with the claims of the writer?

Directions: *In the boxes below, write:*

  NO *if the statement contradicts the claims of the writer;*

  YES *if the statement agrees with the claims of the writer;*

  NOT GIVEN *if it is impossible to say what the writer thinks about this.*

☐ 1. Attitudes towards bilingualism have changed in recent years.

☐ 2. Bilingual people are better than monolingual people at guessing correctly what words are before they are finished.

☐ 3. Bilingual people consistently name images faster than monolingual people.

☐ 4. Bilingual people's brains process single sounds more efficiently than monolingual people in all situations.

☐ 5. Fewer bilingual people than monolingual people suffer from brain disease in old age.

Part 2 Which paragraph contains the following information?

Directions: *Write the correct number, 1-7, in the boxes below.*

☐ 1. an example of how bilingual and monolingual people's brains respond differently to a certain type of non-verbal auditory input

☐ 2. a demonstration of how a bilingual upbringing has benefits even before we learn to speak

☐ 3. a description of the process by which people identify words that they hear

☐ 4. reference to some negative consequences of being bilingual

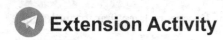

Extensive Reading 2

Extension Activity

Directions: *Choose one topic about language learning from the following list and write an essay of 150-200 words on it.*

1. The Influence of Bilingualism on Creativity and Problem-Solving
2. The Effectiveness of Language Learning Apps
3. The Impact of Technology on Language Learning
4. The Joy of Language Learning: A Personal Experience
5. How to Improve Communication Skills through Language Learning

Value Cultivation: Read and Reflect

UN Chinese Language Day marked across world

Xinhua News Agency 2023-04-24

  The United Nations (UN) Chinese Language Day, which falls on April 20th, has been marked across the world with events highlighting the Chinese language and culture.

  In Hanoi, Vietnam, hundreds of people gathered at the Confucius Institute at Hanoi University to explore Chinese calligraphy, painting, cuisine and music in 2023.

  In Bulgaria, a Chinese singing contest and talent show was staged as well. As many as 14 solo performers and four groups from all over the country participated in the event, which was hosted by the Chinese Embassy in Bulgaria.

According to the United Nations statistics, by the end of 2021, more than 180 countries and regions around the world had offered education in the Chinese language.

An educator in Argentina said that in his school, more children are learning Chinese and they think the course is fun.

In Zimbabwe, many young people are choosing to learn the Chinese language amid the increased economic engagement between Zimbabwe and China.

Unit 6

Chinese Culture

Learning Objectives

Types	Lesson A	Lesson B
Reading Skills	Topic and Main Idea	
Theme	Chinese Characters	Chinese Kung Fu
Vocabulary	Traditional Chinese Culture	Traditional Chinese Culture

Extensive Reading 2

Reading Skills

Topic and Main Idea

When you read a paragraph or short passage, you need to understand what the topic and main idea is. To find what the topic of a paragraph is, ask yourself: What is the paragraph generally about? To find out what the main idea of a topic is, ask yourself: What does the writer say about this topic?

If you can answer these two questions, you are able to find out what the topic and main idea is for a paragraph or short passage.

Topic:

Topic is the subject matter of a discussion. Through reading, most effective readers can find out the *focus* of the writing. Look at the example below.

Example:

Alcohol is a depressant and can lessen a person's normal inhibitions. Because people may feel more free to act in certain ways when drinking, they may think that the drug is a stimulant. It is not, but the excitement of feeling "free" certainly can be. During the euphoric period, a person's diminished self-control can result in social embarrassment, injury, or automobile accidents. Prolonged and excessive use of alcohol can damage the brain, liver, and other internal organs and can change the personality of the alcoholic.

1. What is the topic of the paragraph?

   Alcohol.

2. What aspect of alcohol is the author discussing?

   What alcohol is and its effects on a person.

3. What main idea does the author want you to know about?

   Alcohol is a depressant and can lessen a person's normal inhibitions.

   The main idea in this paragraph is found in the first sentence (a stated topic sentence).

Exercise: Give the topic for each of the following passages.

1. With thousands of years of accumulated cultural snippets to sift through, an outsider cannot hope to catch every potential pitfall. The Chinese language is filled with embarrassing puns and unlucky homonyms that at best can cause snickers behind a foreigner's back. Besides clocks, giving umbrellas is taboo because doing so is homonymous with a phrase that means the person's family will be dispersed. Books, too, are unlucky presents because "giving a book" sounds the same as "delivering defeat".

   Topic: _____

2. Do you have a favorite season? Winter, fall, and spring have many advantages. However, summertime is my favorite season because it offers the tranquility of the beach as well as the exhilaration of outdoor sports. First, sitting on the other side of a sand dune, hidden by sea oats and sedge, I like looking at the Atlantic Ocean, scanning for dolphins and pelicans. Looking at something larger than I am gives me a sense of awe and gratitude and provides a backdrop for some deep musings. Second, summertime provides me with the chance to go sailing, surfing, and hiking along the shore. The exercise enhances a sense of well-being and creates a feeling of optimism.

Topic: _____

3. Body temperature can affect how happily, or unhappily, we awaken. During the course of a day, our body temperature rises and falls at regular times. Although we don't notice the change, it does affect our sleeping patterns. When the body temperature is up, we are awake. As it falls, we grow tired and eventually, we sleep. As a result, anyone who has a fast-rising temperature cycle is a "morning person" and can get out of bed quickly. An "evening person," on the other hand, has a body temperature that rises slowly. It doesn't hit a high point until mid-afternoon., when this person feels best.

Topic: _____

4. Learning to read well is like learning to improve in a sport. There are so many things to think of all at the same time. The inexperienced tennis player, for example, must remember to bend his knees. He must think of keeping his eyes on the ball. He must remember to hold his wrist straight and follow through on his swing. The inexperienced reader also has to remember many things at once. He must try to read in phrases, not word by word. He must analyze new words, look for the main idea, and note-read important details. And at the same time, he must read faster and faster. Both the beginning reader and the tennis player feel frustrated. But practice pays off for the tennis player. Practice will pay off for the reader too and lead to higher and sharper skill. Reading well will become as natural as hitting a ball well.

Topic: _____

5. In America today almost everyone fears aging greatly—and for good reasons. The old are thrown out of the work force at 65, no longer thought useful. They are sent away to retirement villages if they can afford them, to nursing homes if they cannot. One study shows at least one-third of the 22.5 million people over 65 are poor. Most are alone, poor and bitter. A burden to their children, many old people live out their last years hopelessly or angrily. "The poor old folks," we say with pity and fear.

Topic: _____

Main Ideas

The main idea is sometimes contained within a text, so how will you separate it from a paragraph or an article? Do you think the methods of identifying the main idea and finding supporting details are the same in

Extensive Reading 2

a story and an informational text?

In dealing with different reading materials, the ways to summarize main idea or locate the supporting details are different. Here we only take **narrative** and **exposition** as examples.

Narrative

As to narrative writing, a story mapping strategy is very effective. The general idea of story mapping strategy is to find out characters, setting, plot and conclusion of a story and then summarizing the main idea of the story.

Exposition

In expository writing, the main idea of a passage or reading is the central thought or message. Main ideas help readers remember important information. The main idea of a paragraph tells the topic of the paragraph. The topic tells what all or most of the sentences are about. The other sentences in the paragraph are called details. Details describe or explain the main idea.

Example:

The rain forest is home to many creatures. Monkeys, toucans and macaws live in the rain forest. Blue Morpho butterflies and anteaters also live in the rain forest.

The main idea of the paragraph is "The rain forest is home to many creatures". "*Monkeys, toucans and macaws*" or "*Blue Morpho butterflies and anteaters*" are just details to illustrate the point.

Lesson A

Before Reading

Directions: *Look at the following chart and learn something about the evolution of Chinese characters.*

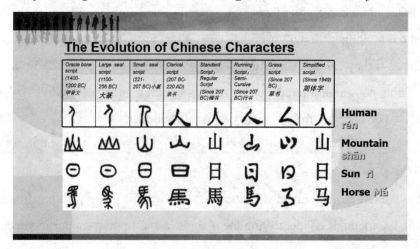

Unit 6 Chinese Culture

While Reading

Write down your starting time and ending time, and then calculate your reading rate.

Starting Time: _____   Ending Time: _____

The Origin and Development of Chinese Characters

¹ Chinese characters have a history of more than several thousand years. As an old and sophisticated form of writing, it is still used by about one-fifth of the world's population. Chinese characters have gone through a number of stages in its development. As one of man's greatest cultural achievements, Chinese characters are the root of Chinese civilization and carrier of Chinese history.

Origin of Chinese Characters

² Where Chinese characters come from still remains a mystery. Based on the ancient Chinese documents and some archaeological discoveries, there are at least three major theories about the origin of Chinese characters.

³ The first one is Cang Jie's invention of Chinese characters. Cang Jie, a legendary figure, is said to be the historiographer of Yellow Emperor and the inventor of the earliest Chinese characters. Legend described him as a great hero with four eyes and two pupils in each eye. He was a good observer and was inspired by the climate, the shapes of objects, the marks and footprints of birds and other animals to record objects.

⁴ The second one is the Eight Trigrams. The Eight Trigrams which is said to be invented by the immortal Fuxi, is also considered as one of the versions concerning the origin of Chinese characters.

⁵ The third one is the picture theory. Modern scholars believe that Chinese characters which began as

Extensive Reading 2

simple drawings of natural objects originated from pictures, such as the Chinese characters "日" "人" "女" "口" "木" "山" "马" "飞". They are pictographic and considered to be the earliest forms of Chinese written symbols.

Square-shaped Chinese Characters

6 Present-day Chinese characters which evolved from ancient characters are well known as square characters. Different from the alphabetic scripts which are spelt in letters, Chinese characters are written in a square space with strokes and radicals. A Chinese radical is a graphical component with either semantic or phonetic indication. And strokes are the smallest unit of a character and are combined together in a certain order indicating the way a Chinese character is written. The general rules for the stroke order are as follows: from top to bottom, from left to right, horizontal going before vertical, from outside to inside and so on. There is no doubt that learning those rules is of great help for Chinese writing. They facilitate learners' memorization and ease the learning process.

Pictographic and Ideographic

7 Chinese characters are pictographic. The alphabetic scripts have nothing to do with any physical objects in the world. However, Chinese characters, originating from basically pictorial representations of objects, are the pictographs created by drawing a sketch to depict a material object or outlining the rough shape of things with simple lines. About 600 Chinese characters among the oldest characters are pictographs which are the drawings associated with the objects they represent. Hence, the pictograph is the basis of Chinese characters.

8 Chinese characters are ideographic. This feature can never be found in alphabetic languages. According to dictionaries, ideogram is a graphic symbol that represents thought, idea or conception, such as the characters "凹" and "凸". Ideograms convey their semantic messages by means of pictorial resemblance to the physical objects. So, different from the alphabetic scripts, Chinese characters are a combination of pronunciation, form and meaning.

Simplified Versus Traditional Chinese

9 At present, the Chinese writing system involves two forms of writing: the simplified Chinese and the traditional Chinese. The simplified Chinese, developed by the People's Republic of China in the 1950s for promoting mass literacy, is a standardized character set used in Chinese mainland. At that time, approximately 2,000 Chinese characters were transformed from their original forms, in the belief that simplified characters would be easier to read and write. Different from simplified Chinese, the traditional Chinese is widely used in China's Taiwan Province, Hong Kong SAR, etc.

International Influence

10 Chinese characters are not only used in China, but also in Japan, Republic of Korea and other Asian countries. In ancient times, the Chinese character was the only script used in Japanese and Korean writing

systems. Evidence still survives in their ancient political documents. And even today a number of Chinese characters are still in use in the languages of those neighboring countries. What's more, the vocabulary and grammatical rules of Chinese have been deeply embedded in those languages in an indirect way. The Chinese language also exerts influence on other languages whose speakers live far away from us. Yang and Yin in the English language are vivid examples of that. As more and more Chinese work and live in other countries of the world, Chinese naturally affects English and other European languages through frequent cultural communication and business cooperation.

(Introducing Chinese Culture in English Unit 3;
791 words; suggested reading time: 6 minutes)

Reading Comprehension

Directions: *Answer the following questions.*

1. What is the pictogram for Chinese character? Can you cite some examples to illustrate?
2. What is the ideogram for Chinese character? Can you cite some examples to illustrate?
3. What are the three major theories about the origin of Chinese characters?

Word Formation

Directions: *Fill in each of the blanks with the given word in its proper form.*

1. There are clear _____ that the economy is improving. (indicate)
2. People who have no knowledge of computer applications are said to be computer _____. (literate)
3. These paints can be used individually or in _____. (combine)
4. The movie bears little _____ to the original novel. (resemble)
5. The character "王" is composed of one vertical and three _____ strokes. (horizon)
6. The way in which we work has undergone a complete _____ in the past decade. (transform)
7. They have given up hope of finding any more _____. (survive)
8. _____ should not be stressed at the expense of comprehension. (memorize)
9. The skyscraper stands _____, towering over the city skyline with its impressive height. (vertical)
10. The information should finally be systematized and _____. (standard)

After Reading

Group Presentation

Directions: *If you were given a chance to teach your foreign friends one single Chinese character, which one*

Extensive Reading 2

would you choose? How would you explain it? Discuss in your group and make a decision about the choice of the character. Your presentation should at least include the pronunciation, part of speech, meaning and usage of the word.

Lesson B

The Principles and Characteristics of Chinese *Kung Fu*

1   Rooted in the war between man and animals in the primitive society, Chinese *kung fu* has a long history. During the progression, some philosophical theories were absorbed by various schools as principles. It also integrated the extrinsic body with the intrinsic soul through the circulation of *qi* and achieved the goal that mind leads *qi* and *qi* promotes strength.

2   Force, fist position, strength and psychology are usually considered to be the four factors of measuring Chinese *kung fu*, which lead to the four principles. That is, force should be hard and pliable; fist position should be hidden; strength should be based on will; and psychology should be in a good state—one should be prepared to fight, but never act upon anger.

3   In Chinese *kung fu*, the basic requirement is an appropriate balance between hardness and softness, and a combination of external and internal forces, also called yang and yin. Pure hard fist may lead to exhaustion of strength and pure soft fist may result in weak strength. Thus, only a balance between hardness and softness can allow the fist to move smoothly.

⁴ For the fist position, Chinese *kung fu* advocates that cats hide their paws. It means the smartest thing seems stupid and simple, which best interprets the discipline of Chinese *kung fu*—neither complicated nor beautiful, but practical. The beautiful fist positions may not be better than the simple ones but the simple positions can exceed beautiful ones. Therefore, the mystery of Chinese *kung fu* does not lie in its fighting techniques because the smartest fighting technique is following no technique, which indicates the essence of Chinese *kung fu*—no technique.

⁵ The third principle is to fight by using will to cultivate *qi* or energy to hit the opponent. The energy is transferred throughout the body by willpower to the utmost extent and is focused on one particular point when the great force is released in a flash. This can be called "strength comes from will" "force derives from mind" or "fist works as desired".

⁶ The psychological principle of Chinese *kung fu* is keeping calm and remaining undaunted. Chinese philosopher Laozi said that "a good fighter is never angry". It implies that *kung fu* learners must be good at adjusting their moods and never act upon anger. An easily irritated man will never be good at Chinese *kung fu*.

⁷ The four principles are deeply rooted in traditional Chinese philosophy. The philosophy has also contributed much to the unique characteristics of Chinese *kung fu*. This can be seen from two of the main characteristics of *kung fu*—the cultivation of extrinsic and intrinsic values and the integration of body and mind.

⁸ Chinese *kung fu* is systematic and is characterized by philosophical connotations. Though it contains many schools, all belong to a large and complete system. It takes the yin and yang and Five Elements theories as its philosophical basis. It regards the harmony between body and mind and harmony between fist fighting techniques and the law of nature as the ultimate destination. The theories on fist fighting techniques represent a complementary integration of Confucianism, Buddhism and Daoism. The practice of *kung fu* strengthening internal organs mainly borrows ideas from traditional Chinese medicine and the Daoist practices of preserving health. Thus, Chinese *kung fu* is actually an ingenious blend of philosophy, medicine, the art of attack and defense, strategies and tactics, and practices of maintaining good health; all these constitute a large and profound theoretical system of *kung fu*.

⁹ Chinese *kung fu* attaches great importance to gradualness, so a *kung fu* man has to follow a strict procedure and no shortcuts are recommended. The practice of *kung fu* should follow three stages: cultivating essence into energy or *qi* (to achieve visible strength), *qi* into spirit (to achieve invisible strength), and spirit into void (to achieve refined strength). From the primary stage which concentrates on basic techniques and develops strong strength to the intermediate stage, eliminating strong strength but cultivating soft strength, until the senior stage, combining fist fighting techniques and the law of nature, the process is based on ancient

Extensive Reading 2

combat techniques and the Daoist practice of health preservation.

¹⁰ What's more, Chinese *kung fu* advocates nurturing *qi* and cultivating morality. It means cultivating *qi*, integrating the law of nature, developing civil and military capabilities, and going against aggression and violence. *Qi* is harmonious with rationality and fist fighting techniques with the law of nature. Nurturing *qi* aims to reach taihe (grand peace) and impartiality, neither too hard nor too soft. And it is against emulative thoughts. The more prosperous the *qi* is, the weaker the emulative thoughts become. Chinese *kung fu* is considered a combination of moral cultivation and physical fitness. It gives priority to *kung fu* ethics, requiring practitioners not to make trouble and bully others, but to help others with a just cause and curb the violent to assist the weak.

¹¹ Chinese *kung fu* also displays an aesthetic sense in diversified styles, which can be seen in the attack and defense movements. These movements show a unique rhythmic beauty as they combine hard and soft strength, and dynamic and static movements. For instance, some fist fighting techniques are quick-paced, stretched, and masculine, while others are elegant and full of femininity. The *baguazhang* and *tai chi* display a beauty of masculinity and firmness, as well as femininity and softness. However, the combat function always takes the first place and dominates the development of Chinese *kung fu*, and the aesthetic value is secondary and occupies a subordinate position. This has been reflected by the development of Chinese *kung fu*. It has experienced a simple-to-complex process, followed by a complex-to-simple process. In its early stage, Chinese *kung fu* was simple and didn't have so many boxing schools and techniques. During the Song, Yuan and Ming dynasties, numerous schools thrived and various boxing techniques emerged. In the Qing Dynasty, the contents and exercises tended to be concise and practical.

¹² In a word, Chinese *kung fu* is one of the valuable forms of traditional Chinese culture. The four factors of force, strength, fist position, and psychology are the disciplines of Chinese *kung fu*. The four features of being systematic, being gradual, being moral and being aesthetic distinguish Chinese *kung fu* from other combat techniques. Its unique principles and characteristics reflect the crystallization of Chinese people's wisdom. With its unique techniques and approaches, Chinese *kung fu* has successfully appeared on the world combat stage.

(*Introducing Chinese Culture in English Unit 14;* 1092 words; suggested reading time: 8 minutes)

 Reading Comprehension

Part 1 Each of the following statements contains information given in one of the paragraphs in the passage. Identify the paragraph from which the information derived and put the corresponding number in the boxes provided.

☐ 1. Chinese *kung fu* displays the beauty of masculinity and femininity.

☐ 2. The basic principles of Chinese *kung fu* are given.

☐ 3. Chinese *kung fu* is systematic and contains many schools.

☐ 4. Acquiring Chinese *kung fu* follows three stages and has no shortcuts.

☐ 5. The psychological principle of Chinese *kung fu* is explained.

☐ 6. Chinese *kung fu* is a combination of moral cultivation and physical fitness.

Part 2 Decide whether the statements are true (T) or false (F) according to the passage.

☐ 1. Chinese *kung fu* has a profound philosophical basis.

☐ 2. In Chinese *kung fu*, the force should be hard enough so as to defeat the opponent.

☐ 3. Chinese *kung fu* is a form of Chinese civilization and the crystallization of Chinese people's wisdom.

☐ 4. Chinese *kung fu* in its highest phase has no discipline.

☐ 5. For Chinese *kung fu*, its aesthetic value sometimes comes before functional value.

Extension Activity

Exploring Chinese Cultural Elements in "*Kung Fu* Panda"

Objective: To enhance your understanding of Chinese culture by analyzing the cultural elements present in the animated film "*Kung Fu* Panda".

Instructions:

Watch the movie "*Kung Fu* Panda" (2008) in its entirety.

Pay close attention to the various cultural elements that are represented in the film.

Extensive Reading 2

Identify and describe at least five distinct elements of Chinese culture that you notice. For each element, provide the following:

Description of the element.

How it is depicted in the movie.

Its significance in Chinese culture.

Write a brief analysis (Paras. 1-2) discussing how the cultural elements contribute to the overall narrative and themes of the film.

Value Cultivation: Read and Reflect

The concept of intangible cultural heritage is a relatively recent one, formalized by the United Nations Educational, Scientific and Cultural Organization (UNESCO) through the adoption of the Convention for the Safeguarding of the Intangible Cultural Heritage in 2003. The convention aims to ensure the protection of this heritage, promote awareness of its importance, and encourage its transmission to future generations. Intangible cultural heritage refers to the practices, representations, expressions, knowledge, skills, as well as the instruments, objects, artifacts, and cultural spaces associated with them. Some key aspects of intangible heritage include:

Oral Traditions and Expressions: This includes language, proverbs, riddles, oral literature, epic poetry, and storytelling.

Performing Arts: Such as traditional music, dance, theater, and puppetry.

Social Practices, Rituals, and Festive Events: These are the practices and events that celebrate seasonal cycles, life stages, and other social occasions.

Knowledge and Practices Concerning Nature and the Universe: This encompasses traditional medicine, agriculture, and other knowledge related to the natural environment.

Traditional Craftsmanship: This involves skills and techniques for producing traditional crafts, including textiles, ceramics, metalwork, and more.

The safeguarding of intangible cultural heritage is important because it contributes to cultural diversity and human creativity. It is also a way to maintain cultural identity and promote social cohesion, especially in the face of globalization and rapid social change.

Question: Can you cite some examples of intangible cultural heritage elements that have been recognized by UNESCO?

Unit 7

Tourism

Learning Objectives

Types	Lesson A	Lesson B
Reading Skills	Organization Patterns (I)	
Theme	Scope of Tourism	Tourism in China
Vocabulary	Tourism	Tourism Attractions in China

Reading Skills

Organization Patterns (I)

The term "organization pattern" refers to how information is organized in a passage. The structure of a text can change many times in a passage and even within a paragraph. Students are often asked to identify text structures or patterns of organization on reading tests. Also, understanding text structures can help students make and interpret arguments. Therefore, it is important that students should learn to identify various patterns of organization.

Reading skills in this unit and next unit will briefly explain **some commonly used patterns of organization** illustrated with examples.

1. Chronological Order

When information in a passage is organized by the time in which each event occurred, it is organized chronologically. Nonfiction passages that are organized chronologically often contain dates. Fiction passages or narratives are more subtle and are organized chronologically but usually have no dates. A narrative or story is a journey through time, and all of the events are arranged in order of time; therefore, every story has a beginning, middle, and end. Even if an author uses flashbacks, flash-forwards, or otherwise manipulates the time in his or her text, the events still occur along a timeline. Stories require the passage of time; therefore, all stories are organized chronologically. Sometimes time will stop in a narrative. Certain passages in a story may focus on describing scenery or spaces, and use a descriptive or spatial method of organization. The conflict of a story may be discussed in terms of problem and solution or cause and effect, but the text in a story is still mainly organized chronologically.

Example:

This morning was crazy. My alarm clock was set for PM instead of AM, so I woke up really late. I just threw on some clothes and ran out the door. I rode my bike as fast as I could and thought that I was going to be late for sure, but when I got there everyone was outside and there were fire trucks all lined up in front of school. I guess somebody pulled the fire alarm before class started. It worked out though, because nobody really noticed or minded that I was tardy.

2. Process Writing

Process writing is when information in a passage is organized by the order in which it occurs. This method of organizing text is generally used for instructions or directions, but it can also be used to explain processes in nature or society, such as how a president is elected.

Process writing is frequently confused with chronological order. To further confound the issue, sometimes people refer to chronological order as chronological sequence. But there is a key difference that distinguishes the two patterns: texts organized chronologically occur at a specific time and setting, whereas texts describing processes or sequences do not occur at any specific time and place. To elaborate, if I tell the story of how I came home and made cookies, that information is organized chronologically. The story took place in my kitchen sometime in the past.

Alternately, consider instructions on how to make cookies. When did that occur? That could happen at any time or no time at all. This is because a recipe describes a process or sequence, one which is not attached to any specific chronology. Unlike chronologically ordered texts, information organized sequentially does not occur at any specific time but, rather, anytime.

Signal Words: First, next, before, lastly, then

Example:

How to Make Cookies. First, get your materials. Then, make your dough. Lastly, cook your dough at 400 degrees for 10 minutes.

3. Spatial Organization

Spatial organization is when information in a passage is organized in order of space or location. If you were to describe the room in which you were sitting right now, you would be using spatial organization. Spatial organization may be also called descriptive writing.

Spatial organization is generally easy to identify but be aware that spatial organization is used in both fiction and nonfiction texts. Most fictional passages are organized chronologically, but in paragraphs where the narrator is describing a setting or the appearance of a character, the information may be organized spatially.

Example:

Volcanoes are a feared and destructive force for good reason. A volcano is like a pressure valve for the inner earth, but they can also be very beautiful. One part of the volcano that people rarely see is the magma

Extensive Reading 2

chamber. The magma chamber is way beneath the Earth's bed rock. It is tremendously hot. Running from the magma chamber to the crater of the volcano is the conduit. The conduit connects the magma chamber to the outer world. At the top of the volcano is the crater. This is where the magma exits. Volcanoes are a beautiful yet dangerous natural phenomenon.

Some **signal words** that might indicate that the writer or speaker is following the spatial pattern of organization include a wide sweeping array of prepositions, some of which are: **next to, behind, across from, below that, above that, to the right of** and so forth.

Exercises: Work out a mind-map of the organization pattern for each example above.

Lesson A

Before Reading

Brainstorming

1. List the tourism destinations you have been to and choose one to describe.
2. List the tourism destinations you desire to visit and explain why.

While Reading

Write down your starting time and ending time, and then calculate your reading rate.

Starting Time: _____   Ending Time: _____

The Context Meaning and Scope of Tourism

1   Travel has existed since the beginning of time, when **primitive** men set out, often **traversing** great

distances in search of game, which provided the food and clothing necessary for his **survival**. Throughout the course of history, people have travelled for purposes of trade, religious **conviction**, economic gain, war, migration and other equally **compelling** motivations. In the Roman era, wealthy aristocrats and high government officials also travelled for pleasure. Seaside resorts located at Pompeii[①] and Herculaneum[②] afforded citizens the opportunity to escape to their vacation villas in order to avoid the summer heat of Rome. Travel, except during the Dark Ages, has continued to grow and, throughout recorded history, has played a vital role in the development of civilizations and their economies.

2 Tourism in the mass form as we know it today is a distinctly twentieth-century phenomenon. Historians suggest that the **advent** of mass tourism began in England during the Industrial Revolution with the rise of the middle class and the availability of relatively inexpensive transportation. The creation of the commercial airline industry following the Second World War and the **subsequent** development of the jet aircraft in the 1950s **signaled** the rapid growth and expansion of international travel. This growth led to the development of a major new industry: tourism. In turn, international tourism became the concern of a number of world governments since it not only provided new employment opportunities but also produced a means of earning foreign exchange.

3 Tourism today has grown significantly in both economic and social importance. In most industrialized countries over the past few years the fastest growth has been seen in the area of services. One of the largest segments of the service industry, although largely unrecognized as an **entity** in some of these countries, is travel and tourism. According to the World Travel and Tourism Council (1992), "travel and tourism is the largest industry in the world on virtually any economic measure including value-added capital investment, employment and tax contributions". In 1992, the industry's gross output was estimated to be $3.5 trillion, over 12 percent of all consumer spending. The travel and tourism industry are the world's largest employer with almost 130 million jobs, or almost 7 percent of all employees. This industry is the world's leading industrial contributor, producing over 6 percent of the world's national product and accounting for capital investment in excess of $422 billion in direct, indirect and personal taxes each year. Thus, tourism has a **profound** impact both on the world economy and, because of the educative effect of travel and the effects on employment, on society itself.

4 However, the major problems of the travel and tourism industry that have hidden, or **obscured**, its economic impact are the diversity and **fragmentation** of the industry itself. The travel industry includes hotels, motels and other types of accommodation; restaurants and other food services; transportation services

---

① Pompeii, preserved ancient Roman city in Campania, Italy, 14 miles (23 km) southeast of Naples, at the southeastern base of Mount Vesuvius.

② Herculaneum, ancient city of 4,000–5,000 inhabitants in Campania, Italy. It lay 5 miles (8 km) southeast of Naples, at the western base of Mount Vesuvius, and was destroyed—together with Pompeii, Torre Annunziata, and Stabiae—by the eruption of Vesuvius in 79 CE.

and facilities; amusements, attractions and other leisure facilities; gift shops and a large number of other enterprises. Since many of these businesses also serve local residents, the impact of spending by visitors can easily be overlooked or **underestimated**. In addition, Meis (1992) points out that the tourism industry involves concepts that have remained **amorphous** to both analysts and decision makers. Moreover, in all nations this problem has made it difficult for the industry to develop any type of reliable or credible tourism information base in order to estimate the contribution it makes to regional, national and global economies. However, the nature of this very diversity makes travel and tourism ideal vehicles for economic development in a wide variety of countries, regions or communities.

5   Once the exclusive province of the wealthy, travel and tourism have become an **institutionalized** way of life for most of the population. In fact, McIntosh and Goeldner (1990) suggest that tourism has become the largest commodity in international trade for many nations and, for a significant number of other countries, it ranks second or third. For example, tourism is the major source of income in Bermuda, Greece, Italy, Spain, Switzerland and most Caribbean countries. In addition, Hawkins and Ritchie, quoting from data published by the American Express Company, suggest that the travel and tourism industry is the number one ranked employer in the Bahamas, Brazil, Canada, France, (the former) West Germany, Hong Kong, Italy, Jamaica, Japan, Singapore, the United Kingdom and the United States. However, because of problems of definition, which directly affect the statistical measurement, it is not possible with any degree of certainty to provide precise, valid or reliable data about the extent of world-wide tourism participation or its economic impact. In many cases, similar difficulties arise when attempts are made to measure domestic tourism.

(https://IELTSMaterial.com,

780 words, suggested reading time:6 minutes)

Reading Comprehension

Part 1 Match the paragraph.

Directions: *Match each of the following subtitle with the corresponding paragraph. Write the paragraph number in the brackets.*

A. difficulty in recognizing the economic effects of tourism (   )

B. the history of travel (   )

C. the world impact of tourism (   )

D. economic and social significance of tourism (   )

E. the development of mass tourism (   )

Part 2 Decide whether the statements are true (T) or false (F) according to the passage.

Directions: *Read the following statements and decide whether they are TRUE, FALSE or NOT GIVEN.*

TRUE *if the statement in the question matches with the account in the text;*

FALSE *if the statement in the question contradicts the account in the text;*

NOT GIVEN *if the statement in the question has no clear connection with the account in the text.*

☐ 1. The largest employment figures in the world are found in the travel and tourism industry.

☐ 2. Tourism contributes over six percent of the Australian gross national product.

☐ 3. Tourism has a social impact because it promotes recreation.

☐ 4. Two main features of the travel and tourism industry make its economic significance difficult to ascertain.

☐ 5. Visitor spending is always greater than the spending of residents in tourist areas.

☐ 6. It is easy to show statistically how tourism affects individual economies.

Word Match

Directions: *Match the following words with their definitions.*

Group 1: Verbs

1. traverse ( )	A. be made difficult to be seen or heard properly
2. obscure ( )	B. do not realize how large or great it is or will be
3. underestimate ( )	C. go across
4. institutionalize ( )	D. make a gesture or sound in order to send them a particular message
5. signal ( )	E. establish it as part of a culture, social system, or organization

Group 2: Adjectives

1. primitive ( )	A. attractive and interesting
2. compelling ( )	B. showing great intellectual depth and understanding; being very great or intense
3. subsequent ( )	C. having no clear shape or structure
4. profound ( )	D. (something that) happened or existed after the time or event that has just been referred to
5. amorphous ( )	E. belonging to a society in which people live in a very simple way, usually without industries or a writing system

Group 3: Nouns

1. survival ( )	A. a strong belief or opinion
2. conviction ( )	B. living through a dangerous situation in which it was possible that they might die
3. advent ( )	C. a small piece or part of something
4. entity ( )	D. starting or coming into existence
5. fragmentation ( )	E. something that exists separately from other things and has a clear identity of its own

Extensive Reading 2

Word Formation

Directions: *Fill in each of the blanks with the given word in its proper form.*

1. _____ activities might include barbecues on the beach and walking tours of the Old Town. (society)
2. There is a need for greater _____ and choice in education. (diverse)
3. Lack of exercise is also a risk factor for heart disease but it's _____ small when compared with the others. (relative)
4. Fast food restaurants are popular in the United States for quick, _____ meals or snacks. (expensive)
5. There's a feeling among a lot of people that music has become too _____. (commerce)
6. Under these conditions, ethnic family patterns were slowly broken down by an increasingly urbanized, _____ environment. (industry)
7. The project has demanded considerable _____ of time and effort. (invest)
8. There still exist some advantages in their educational system, among which some have _____ value. (educate)
9. They had a large _____ over their nearest rivals. (major)
10. More and more travelers are looking for bed and breakfast _____ in private homes. (accommodate)

Cloze

Directions: *Fill in each blank with the proper form of one of the words given below.*

| especially | increasing | culture | geographical | scenery |
| activity | interval | business | postindustrial | associate |

Modern tourism is an __1__ intensive, commercially organized, __2__-oriented set of __3__ whose roots can be found in the industrial and __4__ West. The aristocratic grand tour of __5__ sites in France, Germany, and __6__ Italy—including those __7__ with Classical Roman tourism—had its roots in the 16th century. It grew rapidly, however, expanding its __8__ range to embrace Alpine __9__ during the second half of the 18th century, in the __10__ between European wars.

After Reading

Directions: *Case Study and Presentation*

After Zibo and its barbecue restaurants became a viral sensation in April, 2024, many observers in the media and online believed the city would share the same fate as other once Internet-famous tourist destinations: one cycle of virality with increased media attention, explosive tourist influx, followed by a quick cool-down, and then return to pre-viral normalcy.

What's the present situation of the tourism in Zibo and other Internet-famous tourist destinations?

How can they achieve the sustainable development of the tourism?

You can work in a group to carry out a case study and deliver a presentation in class.

Lesson B

Write down your starting time and ending time, and then calculate your reading rate.

Starting Time: _____   Ending Time: _____

China Tourism — Current Trends and Facts

¹ Tourism in China has boomed because of its abundant tourist attractions and enhanced tourist environment. More and more foreign tourists are finding China an ideal travel destination. A continued increase in foreign tourists is expected for the next decade.

² Here is some useful information about tourism in China: where tourists go, why tourism in China is so good trends, when tourists travel, and how tourists travel.

Rich Tourist Resources in China: Top Cities and Attractions

³ China covers an area of 9.6 million square kilometers (3.7M sq mi) and has a history of over 5,000 years. Famous historical and cultural sites, beautiful natural scenery, and interesting folk customs draw millions of tourists to China.

Extensive Reading 2

Historical and Cultural Sites

Beijing

4   Beijing is the best place to help you learn about Chinese history during the Ming (1368-1644) and Qing (1644-1912) dynasties because Beijing served as the capital of six ancient dynasties, the most famous of which were those two dynasties.

5   The Forbidden City holds stories of 24 emperors who stayed there during the Ming and Qing dynasties. You can visit the palaces where they lived and worked. Pay a visit to the Summer Palace, which used to be the summer retreat for imperial families.

6   Visit the world's longest wall—the Great Wall, a symbol of the Chinese nation. Learn about its structure—the walls, watchtowers, and fortresses—and why it was built.

Xi'an

7   If you want to know more about China's ancient history, such as the Zhou (1045-221 BC), Han (206 BC-220 AD), or Qin (221-206 BC) dynasties, then go to Xi'an. Serving as the capital city of 13 dynasties, Xi'an is the oldest of China's Four Great Ancient Capitals. It is often called the birthplace of Chinese civilization.

8   You can learn about the history of the first emperor of China by visiting the Terracotta Army. Visit the Big Wild Goose Pagoda, which houses the Buddhist materials that Xuanzang brought back from his epic journey to India.

9   Go to Shaanxi History Museum to feast your eyes as you see large collections ranging from the times of ape-men to the Qing Dynasty before the Opium War in 1839, and from large bronze wares to exquisite golden carvings.

Nanjing

10   In Nanjing, you can learn more about the history of the 1911 revolution.

11   You can visit Ming Xiaoling Mausoleum, the tomb of the Hongwu Emperor, Zhu Yuanzhang, from the Ming Dynasty and one of the largest imperial mausoleums in existence. Go to Dr. Sun Yat-sen's Mausoleum to learn about the great deeds that Sun Yat-sen did for the Chinese revolution around the turn of the 20th century. Visit the Presidential Palace, which used to be the political and military center of China from the First Opium War in 1839 to Nanjing's peaceful liberation in 1949.

Luoyang

12   Luoyang and Xi'an alternated as capital city in the 1,500 years from the Zhou Dynasty (1046-256 BC). During 13 dynasties, 105 emperors set their capitals in Luoyang.

13   can visit the Longmen Grottoes, which hold over 100,000 Buddhist images and statues. Explore White Horse Temple, which is considered to be the cradle of Chinese Buddhism. Visit Luoyang Ancient Tombs

Museum, which is one of the largest museums of ancient tombs in China and the first one in the world. You can learn about the characteristics of typical tombs in Luoyang over a period of 3,000 years.

Natural Sites

Guilin

14   Guilin is reputed as one of the world's most beautiful places with its karst landscapes, clean rivers, idyllic countryside, and majestic rice terraces. Slow down and allow yourself to have a relaxing vacation in Guilin.

15   The Li River winds through limestone peaks, which look like giant bamboo shoots growing out of the green plain. Take a Li River cruise from Guilin to Yangshuo to appreciate the karst landscape. The rice terraces in Longsheng are really beautiful. When all the rice terraces are filled with water and bathed in sunlight, the reflections are magnificent.

Zhangjiajie

16   Zhangjiajie is famous for its precarious peaks, limpid streams, dense forests, and large karst caves.

17   Explore Zhangjiajie National Forest Park where there are breathtaking rock pillars, which form a forest of massive pillars. Take the world's longest cable car ride to Tianmen Mountain to appreciate its towering peaks. After rainfall, the mountain is covered with thin clouds and mist. It is like a fairyland!

The Yellow Mountains

18   Oddly shaped pines twist directly out of the smooth rocks. Strangely shaped rocks make the Yellow Mountains a natural exhibition hall of rocks. The mystical sea of clouds adds an ethereal atmosphere to the Yellow Mountains, making the peaks look like islands in the sky.

19   You can hike up and down the mountains or take a cable car ride to admire the all-inclusive beauty. Explore off the beaten path in West Sea Grand Canyon. A sunrise at the Refreshing Terrace and a sunset at Cloud-Dispelling Pavilion are not to be missed.

Jiuzhaigou

20   Jiuzhaigou is on UNESCO's World Heritage List. It is famous for its stunning natural scenery of colorful lakes, mature forests, and spectacular waterfalls. The beautiful scenery attracts many photographers.

21   You can see beautiful alpine reeds swaying in the breeze in Reed Lake. See smooth blue water surrounded by dense trees gleaming under the sunlight in Sparking Lake. The reflected light jumps and flashes on the lake. Go to Five-Color Pond where the lake blazes with colors, such as green, light blue, and gray.

Folk Customs

Guizhou

22   Guizhou is located in Southwest China. Many minority groups live in Guizhou, including the Miao,

Extensive Reading 2

Dong, Shui, and Gejia.

23 Visiting an ethnic village is a good way to learn about the local customs. You can learn about their traditional handicrafts, such as batik in Matang Gejia Village and papermaking in Shiqiao Miao Village. You can also take part in the Miao New Year Festival (usually from October to November). The Miao people will dress up and parade to a neighboring village, worship ancestors, and perform antiphonal singing.

Xizang

24 You can immerse yourself in the local culture in Xizang. There are many Buddhist buildings there due to the local people's strong culture of faith. You can go to the Potala Palace, a testament to the local people and their beliefs, visit Jokhang Temple, the spiritual center of Tibet, and visit Yamdrok Lake.

Kashgar

25 The city of Kashgar has the most Uyghur characteristics. You can go to Kashgar Old City, the only traditional historical block with typical characteristics of ancient western regions that has been preserved in China. Visit Abakh Khoja Tomb to learn about the Islamic mazar (shrine) culture. Walk along Handicraft Street, which has an amazing range of handicrafts, including copper, metal, porcelain, woodwork, and other types of goods.

(https://www.chinahighlights.com,

1125 words, suggested reading time: 9 minutes)

Reading Comprehension

Direcitons: *Decide whether each of the following statements is true or false.*

☐ 1. The Forbidden City holds stories of 24 emperors who stayed there during the Ming and Qing dynasties.

☐ 2. Ming Xiaoling Mausoleum, the tomb of the Yongle Emperor, Zhu Di, from the Ming Dynasty and one of the largest imperial mausoleums in existence.

☐ 3. During 13 dynasties, 105 emperors set their capitals in Luoyang.

☐ 4. Shaolin Temple is considered as the cradle of Chinese Buddhism.

☐ 5. Jiuzhaigou is on UNESCO's World Heritage List.

☐ 6. Visiting an ethnic village is a good way to learn about the local customs.

☐ 7. There are many Taoist buildings in Xizang due to Xizang's strong culture of faith.

☐ 8. Kashgar Old City is said to be the only traditional historical block with typical characteristics of ancient western regions that has been preserved in China.

Unit 7 Tourism

 **Extension Activity**

Directions: *Suppose you are a tour guide of a group of foreign tourists who are paying a visit to your hometown. Please write a paragraph to introduce a famous local tourist attraction to them.*

Value Cultivation: Read and Reflect

World Tourism Day 2024: A Global Message of Tourism for Peace

Tourism has committed to embrace its unique role as a pillar of peace and understanding. On World Tourism Day 2024, UN Tourism brought sector leaders from every global region together around a common vision and commitment to building a "peace-sensitive sector", recognizing its potential to build bridges and foster understanding.

The official celebrations in Tbilisi, Georgia, welcomed almost 500 participants from 51 different countries, including 13 Ministers of Tourism. Reflecting its firm commitment to the day and its theme of

Extensive Reading 2

"Peace and Tourism", the host country was represented by Prime Minister Irakli Kobakhidze as well as seven other Ministers, showcasing tourism's cross-sectoral importance.

Welcoming delegates, UN Tourism Secretary-General Zurab Pololikashvili, stressed that "without peace, there is no tourism". He said: "I call on all of you to help build a 'peace-sensitive tourism sector' one that plays a key role in building peace and ending conflicts, provides tourism stakeholders with tools to realize this potential, promotes tourism education as peace education, and links tourism to other peace building initiatives."

(图文来源：https://unwto.org)

Unit 8

Artificial Intelligence

Learning Objectives

Types	Lesson A	Lesson B
Reading Skills	Organization Patterns (II)	
Theme	Artificial Intelligence	Artificial General Intelligence
Vocabulary	Computer Science and Intelligence	Computer Science and Intelligence

Extensive Reading 2

Reading Skills

Organization Patterns (II)

4. Cause and Effect

Cause and effect is a common way to organize information in a text. Paragraphs structured as cause and effect explain reasons why something happened or the effects of something. These paragraphs can be ordered as causes and effects or as effects and then causes. The cause and effect text structure is generally used in expository and persuasive writing modes.

Example:

The dodo bird used to roam in large flocks across America. Interestingly, the dodo wasn't startled by gunshot. Because of this, frontiersmen would kill entire flocks in one sitting. Unable to sustain these attacks, the dodo was hunted to extinction.

Identifying a text written using the cause and effect pattern of organization can be tricky. In most stories, events in the plot occur for various reasons, This can be mistaken for the cause and effect text structure; however, stories are organized chronologically, and the information in each passage is more likely to be organized by the time in which each event occurred. Contrarily, cause and effect passages usually focus on explaining the reason why something occurs or occurred.

Here are some signal words that may indicate that information in a paragraph is organized as cause and effect: **because, as a result, result in, result from, be caused by, be affected by, since, because of, due to, effect, owing to, so, therefore, consequently.**

5. Problem and Solution

Problem and solution is a pattern of organization where information in a passage is expressed as a dilemma or concerning issue (a problem) and something that was, can be, or should be done to remedy this issue (solution or attempted solution).

The problem and solution text structure may seem like it would be easy to recognize, but it can be moderately difficult to identify because it is frequently confused with the cause and effect pattern of organization, as they both have relational structures; however, if you read the passage and look specifically for both a problem and a solution to the problem, you should find it pretty easy to distinguish from cause and effect, as cause and effect passages do not propose solutions to any negative occurrences within the passage but rather just explain why or how they happen.

Example:

Dr. Miller doesn't want the tigers to vanish. These majestic beasts are disappearing at an alarming rate. Dr. Miller thinks that we should write to our congress people. If we let them know that we demand the preservation of this species, maybe we can make a difference. Dr. Miller also thinks that we should donate to Save the Tigers. Our donations will help to support and empower those who are fighting the hardest to preserve the tigers. We owe it to our grandchildren to do something.

6. Compare and Contrast

Compare and contrast is a pattern of organization where the similarities and differences of two or more things are explored. It is important to remember that with the compare and contrast pattern the text should be discussing similarities and differences. If the text only discusses similarities, it is only comparing. Likewise, if it only discusses ways that the things are different, it is only contrasting. The text must do both to be considered compare and contrast.

Example:

Linux and Windows are both operating systems. Computers use them to run programs. Linux is totally free and open source, so users can improve or otherwise modify the source code. Windows is proprietary, so it costs money to use and users are prohibited from altering the source code.

Identifying when the writer is comparing and contrasting is usually not difficult because the speaker will bounce back and forth between two subjects and this pattern is generally pretty easy to recognize. However, here are some signal words that may indicate that the text is written using the compare and contrast organizational pattern: **like, unlike, both, neither, similar,** and **different**.

There are two patterns of compare and contrast: the block pattern and the point-by-point pattern, which can be illustrated as follows:

Extensive Reading 2

The Block Pattern

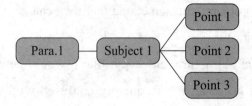

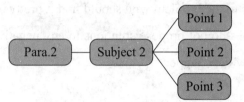

The Point-by-Point Pattern

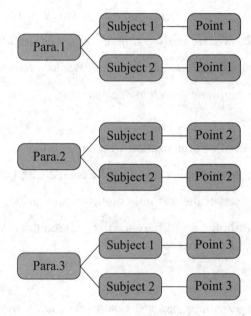

Exercises: Work out a mind-map of the organization pattern for each example above.

Lesson A

Before Reading

Brainstorming

Directions: *Work in pairs and describe the application of AI in your daily life and learning.*

Unit 8 Artificial Intelligence

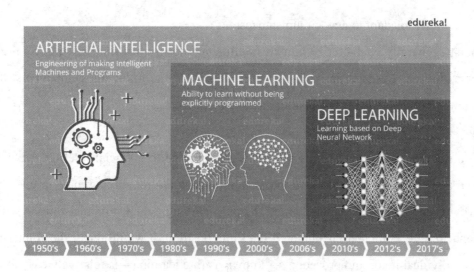

While Reading

Write down your starting time and ending time, and then calculate your reading rate.

Starting Time: _____   Ending Time: _____

Artificial Intelligence (AI): At a Glance

B. J. Copeland

1   All but the simplest human behavior is ascribed to intelligence, while even the most complicated insect behavior is usually not taken as an indication of intelligence. What is the difference? Consider the behavior of the digger wasp, *Sphex ichneumoneus*. When the female wasp returns to her burrow with food, she first deposits it on the threshold, checks for intruders inside her burrow, and only then, if the coast is clear, carries her food inside. The real nature of the wasp's instinctual behavior is revealed if the food is moved a few inches away from the entrance to her burrow while she is inside: on emerging, she will repeat the whole procedure as often as the food is displaced. Intelligence—conspicuously absent in the case of the wasp—

Extensive Reading 2

must include the ability to adapt to new circumstances.

2   Psychologists generally characterize human intelligence not by just one trait but by the combination of many diverse abilities. Research in AI has focused chiefly on the following components of intelligence: learning, reasoning, problem solving, perception, and using language.

Learning

3   There are a number of different forms of learning as applied to artificial intelligence. The simplest is learning by trial and error. For example, a simple computer program for solving mate-in-one chess problems might try moves at random until a mate is found. The program might then store the solution with the position so that, the next time the computer encountered the same position, it would recall the solution. This simple memorizing of individual items and procedures—known as rote learning—is relatively easy to implement on a computer. More challenging is the problem of implementing what is called generalization. Generalization involves applying past experience to analogous new situations. For example, a program that learns the past tense of regular English verbs by rote will not be able to produce the past tense of a word such as *jump* unless the program was previously presented with *jumped*, whereas a program that is able to generalize can learn the "add-*ed*" rule for regular verbs ending in a consonant and so form the past tense of *jump* on the basis of experience with similar verbs.

Reasoning

4   To reason is to draw inferences appropriate to the situation. Inferences are classified as either deductive or inductive. An example of the former is, "Fred must be in either the museum or the café. He is not in the café; therefore, he is in the museum", and of the latter is, "Previous accidents of this sort were caused by instrument failure. This accident is of the same sort; therefore, it was likely caused by instrument failure". The most significant difference between these forms of reasoning is that in the deductive case, the truth of the premises guarantees the truth of the conclusion, whereas in the inductive case, the truth of the premises lends support to the conclusion without giving absolute assurance. Inductive reasoning is common in science, where data are collected and tentative models are developed to describe and predict future behavior—until the appearance of anomalous data forces the model to be revised. Deductive reasoning is common in mathematics and logic, where elaborate structures of irrefutable theorems are built up from a small set of basic axioms and rules.

5   There has been considerable success in programming computers to draw inferences. However, true reasoning involves more than just drawing inferences: it involves drawing inferences *relevant* to the solution of the particular problem. This is one of the hardest problems confronting AI.

Problem-solving

6   Problem-solving, particularly in artificial intelligence, may be characterized as a systematic search

through a range of possible actions in order to reach some predefined goal or solution. Problem-solving methods are divided into special purpose and general purpose. A special-purpose method is tailor-made for a particular problem and often exploits very specific features of the situation in which the problem is embedded. In contrast, a general-purpose method is applicable to a wide variety of problems. One general-purpose technique used in AI is means-end analysis—a step-by-step, or incremental, reduction of the difference between the current state and the final goal. The program selects actions from a list of means—in the case of a simple robot, this might consist of PICKUP, PUTDOWN, MOVEFORWARD, MOVEBACK, MOVELEFT, and MOVERIGHT—until the goal is reached.

7 Many diverse problems have been solved by artificial intelligence programs. Some examples are finding the winning move (or sequence of moves) in a board game, devising mathematical proofs, and manipulating "virtual objects" in a computer-generated world.

Perception

8 In perception the environment is scanned by means of various sensory organs, real or artificial, and the scene is decomposed into separate objects in various spatial relationships. Analysis is complicated by the fact that an object may appear different depending on the angle from which it is viewed, the direction and intensity of illumination in the scene, and how much the object contrasts with the surrounding field. At present, artificial perception is sufficiently advanced to enable optical sensors to identify individuals and enable autonomous vehicles to drive at moderate speeds on the open road.

Language

9 A language is a system of signs having meaning by convention. In this sense, language need not be confined to the spoken word. Traffic signs, for example, form a mini-language, it being a matter of convention that a sign means "hazard ahead" in some countries. It is distinctive of languages that linguistic units possess meaning by convention, and linguistic meaning is very different from what is called natural meaning, exemplified in statements such as "Those clouds mean rain" and "The fall in pressure means the valve is malfunctioning".

10 An important characteristic of full-fledged human languages—in contrast to birdcalls and traffic signs—is their productivity. A productive language can formulate an unlimited variety of sentences.

11 Large language models like ChatGPT can respond fluently in a human language to questions and statements. Although such models do not actually understand language as humans do but merely select words that are more probable than others, they have reached the point where their command of a language is indistinguishable from that of a normal human. What, then, is involved in genuine understanding, if even a computer that uses language like a native human speaker is not acknowledged to understand? There is no universally agreed-upon answer to this difficult question.

Extensive Reading 2

(https://www.britannica.com,
1054 words, suggested reading time: 8 minutes)

Reading Comprehension

Directions: *Answer the following questions.*

1. What's the difference between human intelligence and insects' instinctual behavior?
2. What are the scopes of traits that define human intelligence according to psychologists?
3. What are the two types of learning mentioned in the text?
4. How can inferences be classified?
5. What's the difference between a deductive case and an inductive case?
6. What are the two categories of problem-solving methods?
7. Why is the analysis in perception complicated?
8. Why is the human language different from birdcalls and traffic signs?
9. What can large language models like ChatGPT do?
10. According to the text, what is involved in genuine understanding?

Word Formation

Directions: *Fill in each of the blanks with the given word in its proper form.*

1. The relationship between a parent and a child is _____ and stems from basic human nature. (instinct)
2. He is making sweeping _____ to get his point across. (generalize)
3. At one point in the Metaphysics, Aristotle seems to distinguish between empirical studies and _____ logic. (deduct)
4. Inductive reasoning is based on the process of _____. (induct)
5. It had _____ meaning but can be redefined in the program. (define)
6. This agreement will be _____ in a state treaty to be signed soon. (embed)
7. We are seeking continuous, _____ improvements, not great breakthroughs. (increment)
8. He treated us as _____ individuals who had to learn to make up our own minds about important issues. (autonomy)
9. Protein supplements may overburden some internal organ, thus leading to its _____. (function)
10. The male of the species is almost _____ from the female. (distinguish)

Unit 8 Artificial Intelligence

Cloze

Directions: *Fill in each blank with the proper form of one of the words given below.*

| basis | release | program | immediate | distinguish |
| concern | foundation | math | laboratory | predict |

Prominent examples of modern Natural Language Processing (NLP) are language models that use artificial intelligence(AI) and statistics to __1__ the final form of a sentence on the __2__ of existing portions. One popular language model was GPT-3, from the American AI research __3__ OpenAI, __4__ in June 2020. Among the first large language models, GPT-3 could solve high-school level __5__ problems and create computer __6__. GPT-3 was the __7__ of ChatGPT software, released in November 2022 by OpenAI. ChatGPT almost __8__ disturbed academics, journalists, and others because of __9__ that it was impossible to __10__ human writing from ChatGPT-generated writing.

Glossary

AI	guardrails	prompt
AI ethics	hallucination	quantum computing
algorithm	hyperparameter	reinforcement learning
application programming interface	image recognition	sentiment analysis
big data	large language model	structured data
chatbot	limited memory	supervised learning
cognitive computing	machine learning	token
computer vision	natural language processing	training data
data mining	neural network	transfer learning
data science	overfitting	turing test
deep learning	pattern recognition	unstructured data
emergent behavior	predicative analytics	unsupervised learning
generative AI	prescriptive analytics	voice recognition

101

Extensive Reading 2

After Reading

Directions: *Topics for discussion.*

1. What kinds of challenges AI might bring or have already brought to our society?
2. What are the possible risks of AI?

Lesson B

Write down your starting time and ending time, and then calculate your reading rate.

Starting Time: _____   Ending Time: _____

What Is Artificial General Intelligence?

1   Artificial general intelligence (AGI) is not yet real—it's a hypothetical form of artificial intelligence (AI) where a machine learns and thinks like a human does. Ultimately, it would blur the lines between human and machine. Programming AGI requires the machine to develop a kind of consciousness and self-awareness that has started to appear in innovations like self-driving cars that adapt to roads and passing trucks.

2   We're far from machines simulating a human's full capabilities, and certainly, there are ethical considerations surrounding whether machines should act as humans do. But it's a fascinating concept that the

field of AI has been approaching, so here's a look at what AGI is and some examples of how we can see it in real life.

What Is Artificial General Intelligence?

³ Artificial general intelligence is a hypothetical type of intelligent agent that has the potential to accomplish any intellectual task that humans can. In some cases, it outperforms human capabilities in ways beneficial to researchers and companies.

⁴ Companies such as OpenAI are conducting research to advance AGI and what it means for companies, governments, and humanity alike. AGI works by incorporating logic into the AI and machine learning processes instead of just applying an algorithm so that its learning and development mirrors that of humans.

Artificial General Intelligence (AGI) Vs. Artificial Intelligence (AI)

⁵ Artificial general intelligence (AGI) is theoretical, even though it is in the midst of being produced and launched, and it should be able to perform a range of intelligence without human intervention—at a human level or surpassing it to solve problems.

⁶ On the other hand, artificial intelligence (AI) is available and in practical use today using a combination of machine learning, deep learning, and neural networks to deliver services like chatbots and voice recognition.

AGI Capabilities

⁷ AGI is essentially AI that has cognitive computing capability and the ability to gain complete knowledge of multiple subjects the way human brains can. It does not currently exist; it is simply in the process of being researched and experimented with. If it were able to surpass human capabilities, AGI could process data sets at speeds beyond what AI is currently capable of. Some of these could include:

- the ability to think abstractly
- gathering and drawing from background knowledge of multiple subjects
- common sense and consciousness
- causation—a thorough understanding of cause and effect

⁸ In practice, this could include capabilities that humans have that AI does not, such as sensory perception. AGI could recognize colors and depth. Along with this are fine motor skills, like how a human reaches into their pocket to take out a wallet or cook a meal without burning their fingers on the stove. AGI could also develop creativity: Rather than generating a Renaissance painting of a cat, it could think of an idea to paint several cats wearing the clothing styles of each ethnic group in China to represent diversity.

⁹ More than just a creative mind, painting cats wearing different Chinese dress patterns requires an understanding of different cultures, symbols, and belief systems. AGI systems would need to handle the subtle nuances of each ethnic group and create a new structure for this task using multiple algorithms at once.

Extensive Reading 2

Examples of Artificial General Intelligence

10 While AGI systems are not available just yet, some examples of artificial intelligence are already meeting or exceeding human capabilities. Research and experimentation are currently underway to advance AI into AGI. Some examples of AGI already present in AI systems today include:

❖ Self-driving cars: These cars are guided by AI to recognize that other cars, people, and things like traffic cones or barriers are in their vicinity. Self-driving cars are designed to know when a car is nearby and to react if it is too close. They are also trained to adhere to driving laws and common rules of the road.

❖ Language model GPT: AI systems like ChatGPT can be prompted to generate human language that mimics how humans communicate. Both the input and output for tools like ChatGPT can be flawed. They also cannot simulate human emotion the way that AGI hypothetically could.

❖ Expert systems: An expert system is driven by AI to simulate human judgment. A common example is a health care expert system that prescribes specific types of medicine after reading a patient's records.

❖ IBM's Watson (and other supercomputers): Supercomputers like Watson can calculate faster than the average computer. With the addition of AI, they can carry out tasks such as modeling the birth of the universe.

11 If AGI were to exist, these examples would be able to surpass human intelligence. At the moment, self-driving cars require humans to be present to make decisions when the car's AI capability does not allow it to problem-solve in ambiguous situations.

The Future of Artificial General Intelligence

12 In the future, though, AGI could do all this and more. While some researchers question whether it is viable, or even desirable, it is likely that experts will continue working to develop AGI. AI that operates beyond human capabilities is a point of artificial superintelligence that is sometimes called singularity.

13 AI creations like ChatGPT and DALL-E were recently released to the general public and embraced by everyday users and professionals looking to generate outlines, sample prototypes, or simple lines of code. No matter how AI continues to develop, it is clear that AGI is on the horizon, and technology will advance to include this type of cognitive computing.

(https://www.coursera.org,

914 words, suggested reading time: 7 minutes)

Reading Comprehension

Directions: Answer the following questions.

1. What is this text mainly about?
2. What does programming AGI require machine to develop?
3. Can AGI outperform human?
4. How does AGI work to mirror the human learning process?
5. Summarize the differences between AI and AGI.
6. What are the potential capabilities of AGI in the future?
7. Summarize the capabilities of self-driving cars.
8. What is the working mechanism of the language model GPT?
9. Have the examples mentioned in this text come into reality?
10. What's the author's attitude towards the future of AGI?

 Extension Activity

Directions: The following paragraphs showcase Tim Cook's opinion about AI. Read, reflect and then write an essay of about 300 words.

Tim Cook, the CEO of Apple, has spoken of his fears for the future of the human race under the influence of artificial intelligence (AI), during a sobering commencement address at the Massachusetts Institute of Technology.

"Technology is capable of doing great things, but it doesn't want to do great things," the Apple chief executive said during his speech. "It doesn't want anything. That part takes all of us. It takes our values, and our commitment to our families, and our neighbors, and our communities."

He was not worried about AI giving computers the ability to think like humans, he added. "I'm more worried about people thinking like computers, without values or compassion, without concern for consequences."

Extensive Reading 2

Value Cultivation: Read and Reflect

日新 Constant Renewal

天天更新。努力使自身不断更新，使民众、社会、国家不断更新，持续进步、完善，始终呈现新的气象。它是贯穿在"修齐治平"各层面的一种自强不息、不断革新进取的精神。

This term refers to an ongoing process of self-renewal, which also brings new life to the people, society, and the nation. This process features continuous progress and improvement. It represents a tenacious and innovative spirit that permeates all levels of "self-cultivation, family regulation, state governance, bringing peace to all under heaven".

引例：汤之盘铭曰："苟日新，日日新，又日新。"《康诰》曰："作新民。"《诗》曰："周虽旧邦，其命维新。"是故君子无所不用其极。(《礼记·大学》)

释义：商朝的开国君主汤的浴盆上加铸的铭文说："如果能够一天更新自己，就应保持天天更新，更新了还要再更新。"《尚书·康诰》上说："激励民众弃旧图新，去恶向善。"《诗经》上说："周虽然是古老的国家，却禀受了新的天命。"所以君子无时无处不尽心尽力革新自己。

翻译："If we can improve ourselves in one day, we should do so every day, and keep building on improvement," reads the inscription on the bathtub of Tang, founder of the Shang Dynasty. "People should be encouraged to discard the old and embrace the new, give up evil ideas, and live up to high moral standards," says *The Book of History*. "Though it was an ancient state, Zhou saw its future lying in continuously renewing itself," comments *The Book of Songs*. Therefore, *junzi* (men of virtue) should strive to excel themselves in all aspects and at all times. (*The Book of Rites*)

（图文来源：学习强国平台）